Lighthouses of New Jersey

Michelangelo DeSantis

Copyright © 2019 Michelangelo DeSantis
All rights reserved.
ISBN-13: 978-1727178333

ISBN-10:1727178335

DEDICATION

The book is dedicated to my wife, Denise, who goes along on my crazy trips to photograph these lighthouses.

Contents

Introduction 5
Robbins Reef Light Station 6
Great Beds Light Station 8
Romer Shoal Light Station 10
Conover Beacon 12
Chapel Hill Lighthouse 14
Sandy Hook 16
Twin Lights 18
Sea Girt 20
Barnegat Light 22
Tucker's Island Light 24
Hereford Inlet lighthouse 25
Absecon Lighthouse 28
Cape May 30
Brandywine Shoal 32
East Point Lighthouse 34
Miah Maull 36
Elbow of Cross Ledge 38
Ship John Shoal 40
Finn's Point Rear Range 42
Tinicum Island Rear Range 44
Fresnel Lens 46
National Register of Historical Places 47
About the Author 49

Introduction

There is something that people find fascinating about lighthouses. I'm not sure what draws me to them except for the fact that they are on the coast. I've lived within 20 miles of salt water for most of my life and the idea of living anywhere else has just never occurred to me.

New Jersey is the beneficiary of a long coastline - 125 miles on the Atlantic coast and more than 150 miles of shoreline along the Delaware River and Delaware Bay. In addition, the state borders both Upper and Lower New York Bay and the lower Hudson River. New Jersey boasts 19 original lighthouses and one replica. The lighthouses are as tall as 171 feet and as short as 36 feet and represent many innovations in technology.

Many additional lighthouses and lightships once protected the waters in and around New Jersey. Sadly, the ravages of sea and salt, storms and ice, and neglect have taken their toll. Lights such as Ludlum's Beach, the Fort Mifflin Range Lights, a number of lightships, and others are lost to history although one interesting former lighthouse remains standing - *The Statue of Liberty*.

These sentinels have stood guard over oceans, bays, and rivers since colonial times. Some still operate as aids to navigation while others operate sentimentally. Each has a story to tell and I encourage readers to visit the lighthouses to get more information about the buildings and the people. There is a lot of history contained in these structures and a lot of romance too.

Lighthouses are so loved that August 7 each year is dedicated as National Lighthouse Day. So, sit back, relax, and enjoy this photographic look at the Lighthouses of New Jersey.

Robbins Reef Light Station

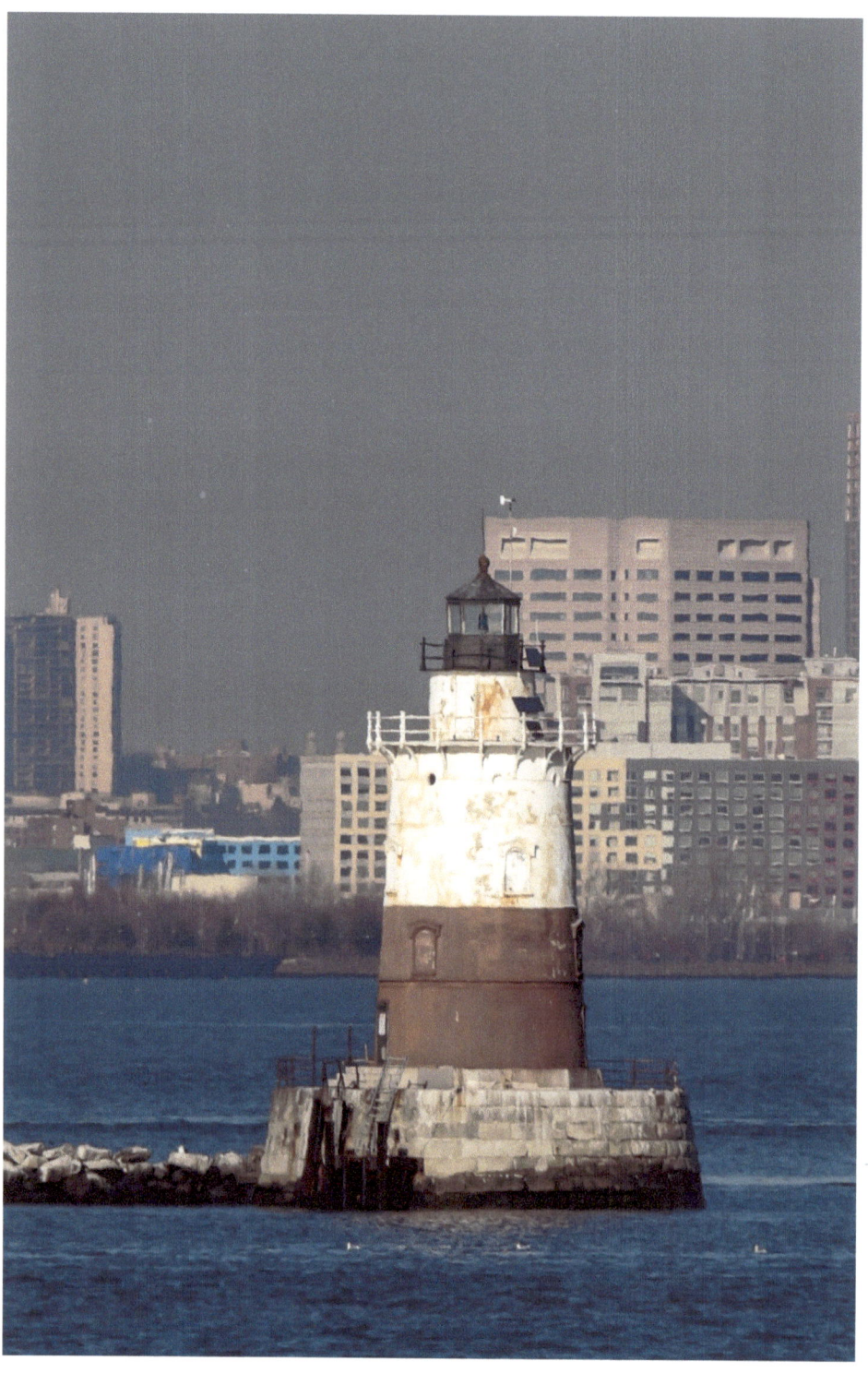

Robbins Reef Light Station is located off Constable Hook part of Bayonne, New Jersey. The light is an example of a sparkplug lighthouse. Sparkplug lighthouses are also known as caisson lighthouses, coffee pot lighthouses, or bug lighthouses. This type of lighthouse was pre-fabricated as a cast iron structure placed on solid foundations in shallow waters. There are 33 of the type remaining in the United States - five are in New Jersey waters. The light station is 46 feet tall and had an original fourth-order Fresnel lens.

A lighthouse was erected on this spot as early as 1839, however, the current structure dates back to 1883. The brick structure next to the light in the below photograph is sometimes mistaken for the location of the original light but is instead a part of a sewage project built in the early 20th century. Today the property is managed by *Noble Maritime Collection*, a maritime museum located on Staten Island, New York. The museum is in the process of restoring the light.

The lighthouse is popularly known as *Kate's Light*, a reference to Katherine Walker. Katherine was a German immigrant who worked at the light for 30 years after the death of her keeper husband Captain John Walker in 1861. Despite here long service, Ms. Walker was only officially named keeper in 1890.

Katherine's name is not just associated with Robbins Reef Light Station. She is the namesake for the United States Coast Guard Coastal Buoy Tender *Katherine Walker* (WLM-552) that is home ported in Bayonne.

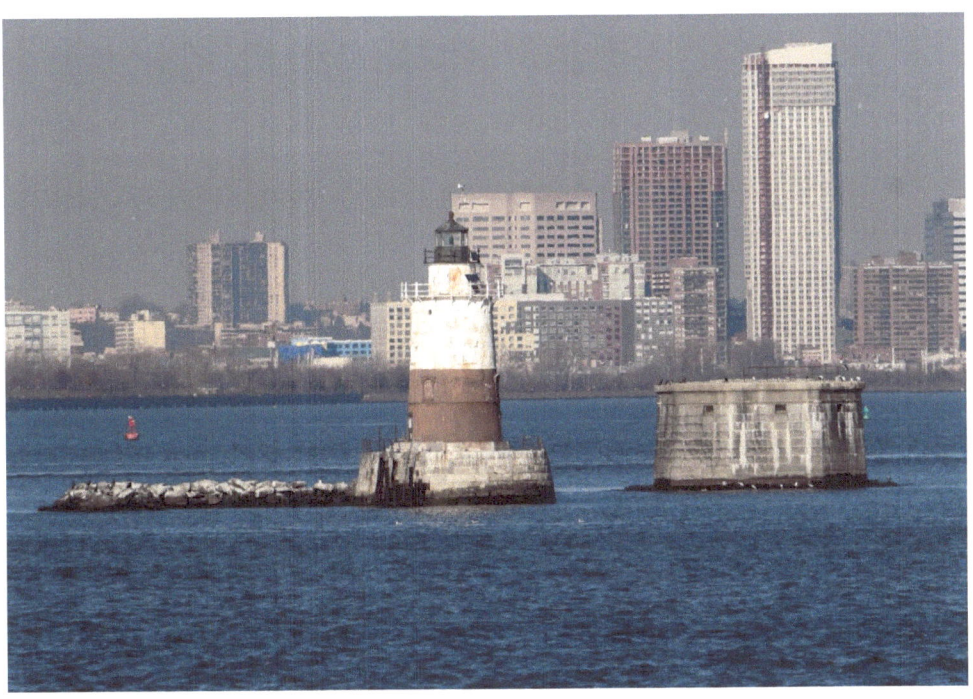

Great Beds Light Station

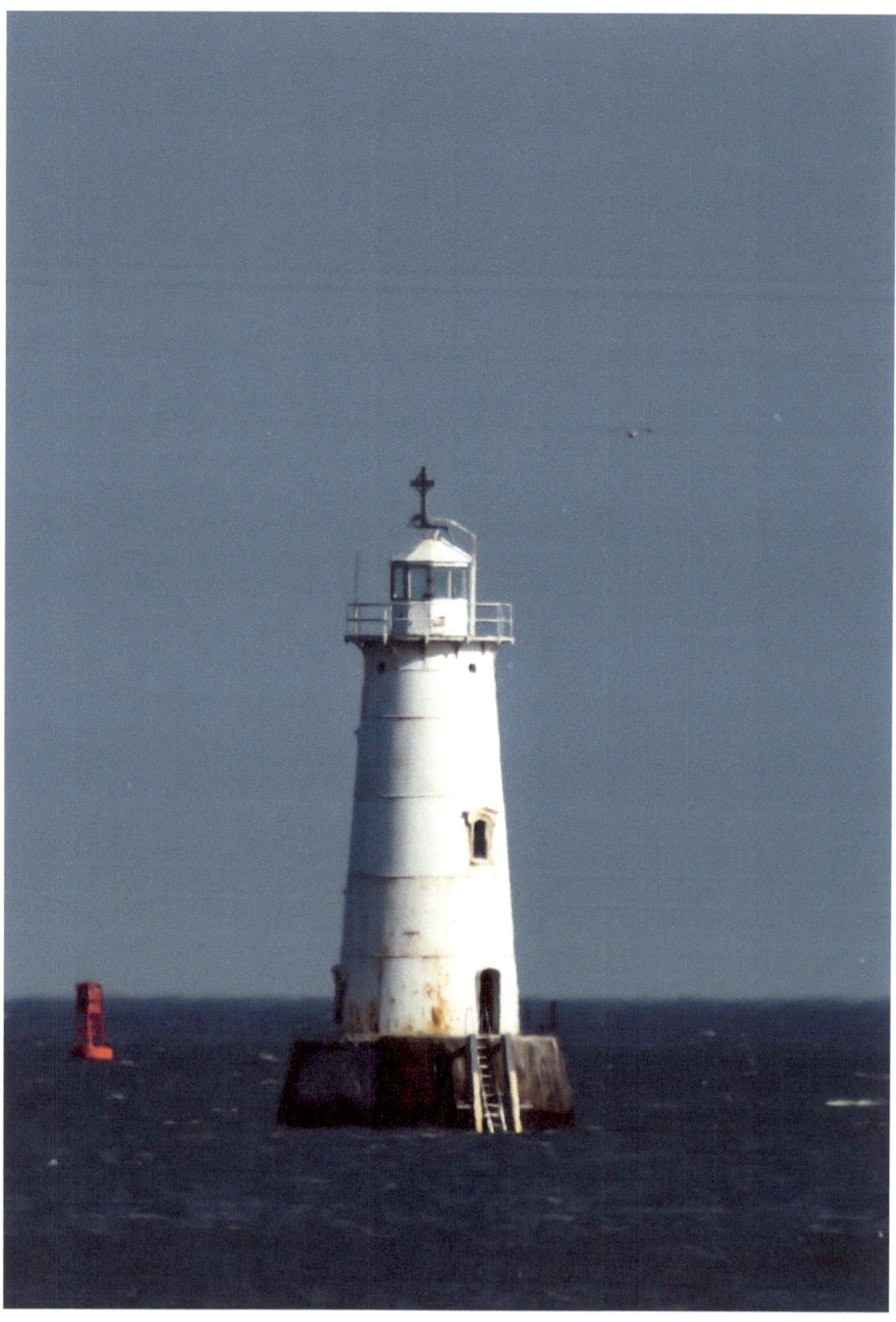

Another sparkplug light. This one is in Raritan Bay. The light is about three-quarters of a mile off the coast of Sayreville in Middlesex County, New Jersey. The lighthouse is located on what was once very active oyster bed hence the name. The current lighthouse replaced a deteriorating lightship that once guarded the shoals.

The actual state in which the lighthouse resides has been the subject of debate. In 1879, the United States Lighthouse Board listed the light in New Jersey and in 1880 the board listed it in New York. In 1898, the Lighthouse Board listed it in both states but subsequent listings have it in New Jersey.

The lighthouse was originally painted red but around 1890 it was painted brown. Its color was changed to the current white coat shortly afterward.

Automation came to the lighthouse in 1945 but by 2010, the Coast Guard declared it surplus and offered it free of charge to eligible organizations. When no eligible organization came forward, the United States government decided to put the light up for auction. After a small number of bids were received, the ownership was transferred to private hands for $90,000.

The lighthouse is a part of the persona of the City of South Amboy. In fact, the light is proudly displayed on the city's seal.

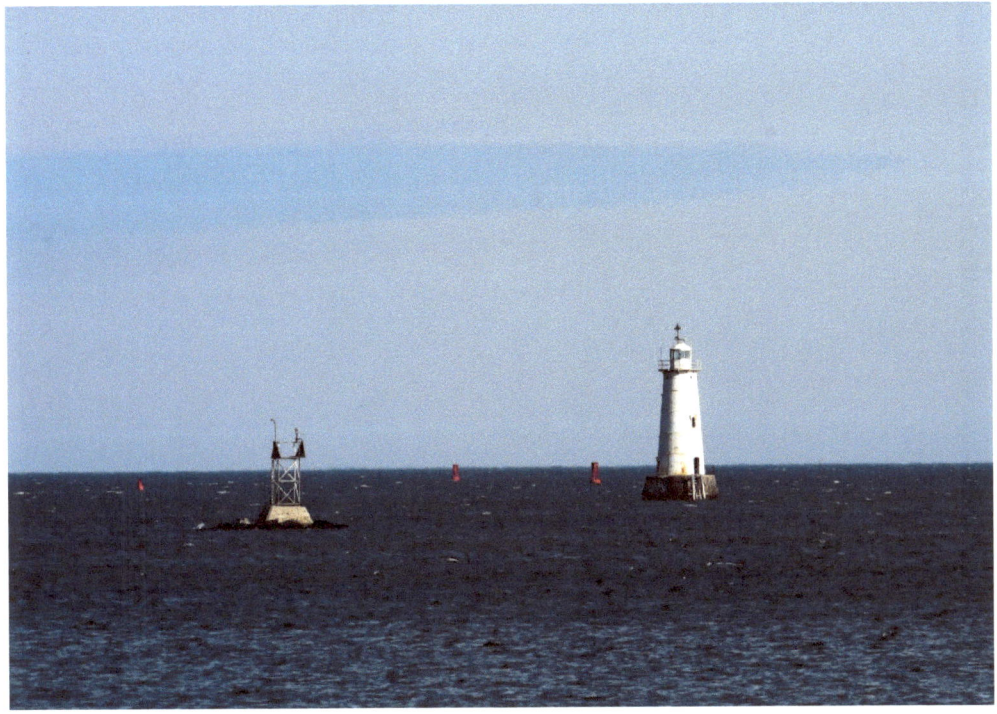

Romer Shoal Light Station

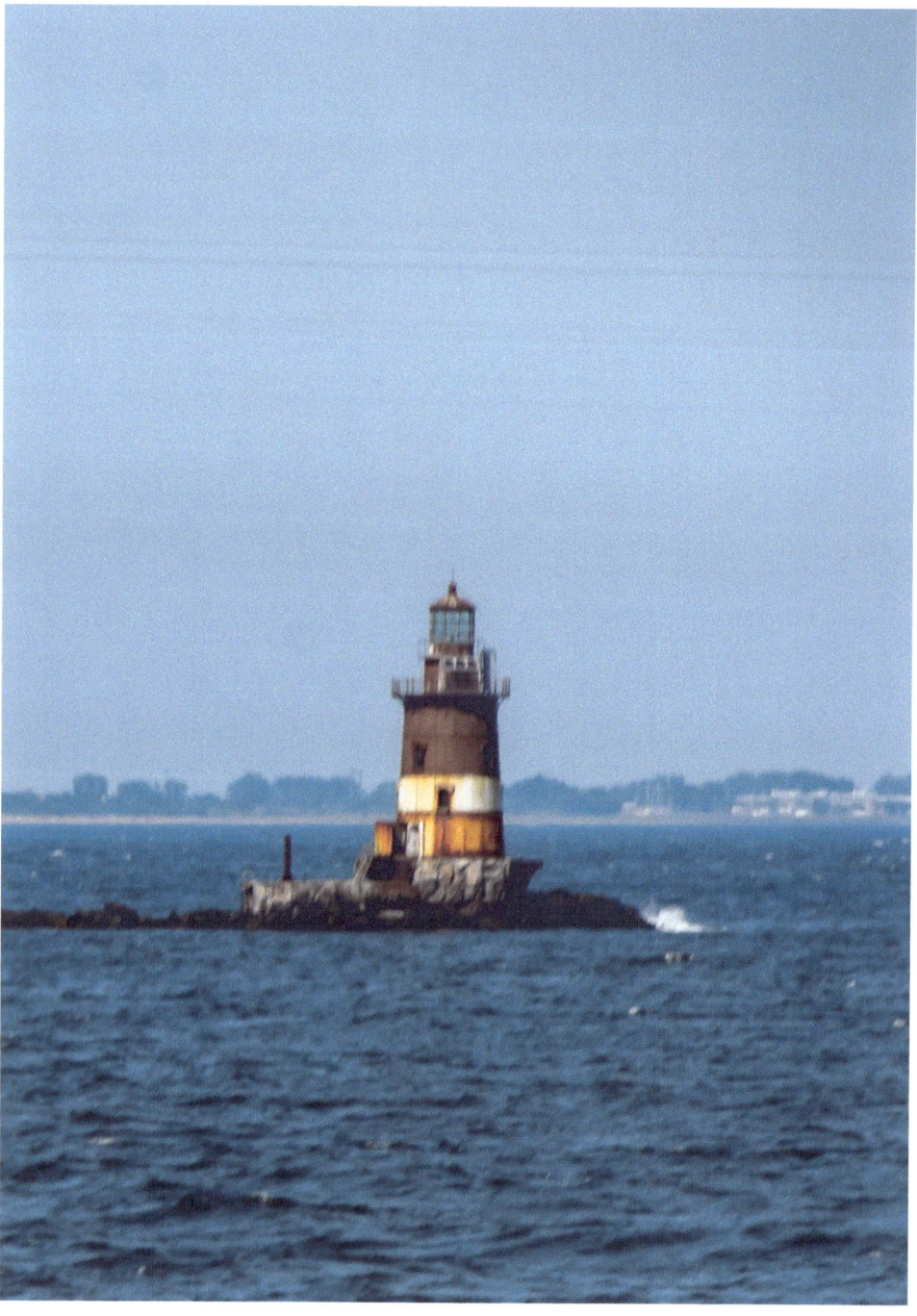

Yet another sparkplug type lighthouse located in Lower New York Harbor. The light is just outside of Ambrose Channel - the major path of entry into New York Harbor. This light has been in the current location since 1898 although a light has marked the shoals since 1838. Current GPS coordinates say the lighthouse is in New York waters but the lighthouse is acknowledged to be in New Jersey waters.

The shoal is named for Colonel Wolfgang William Romer a Dutch military engineer who did nautical surveys of the area. A myth persists that says that the shoal is named after a ship, the *William J. Romer* that sank in 1863 on the spot. However, research shows that the *William J. Romer* sank about 50 miles from the reef where the light is located.

The light is 54 feet tall and originally had a fourth-order Fresnel lens. The current optics are a 7.5 inch (190 mm) lens that is visible for 15 miles. The light was automated in 1966 and solar power was added to the station in 1997. The tower is on a concrete base in a cast iron caisson.

Damaged by a storm in 1992, the light was almost scrapped save for the efforts of local enthusiasts. Severely damaged again in the 2012 Superstorm Sandy, volunteers are attempting to restore the structure. Their work and fundraising efforts continue.

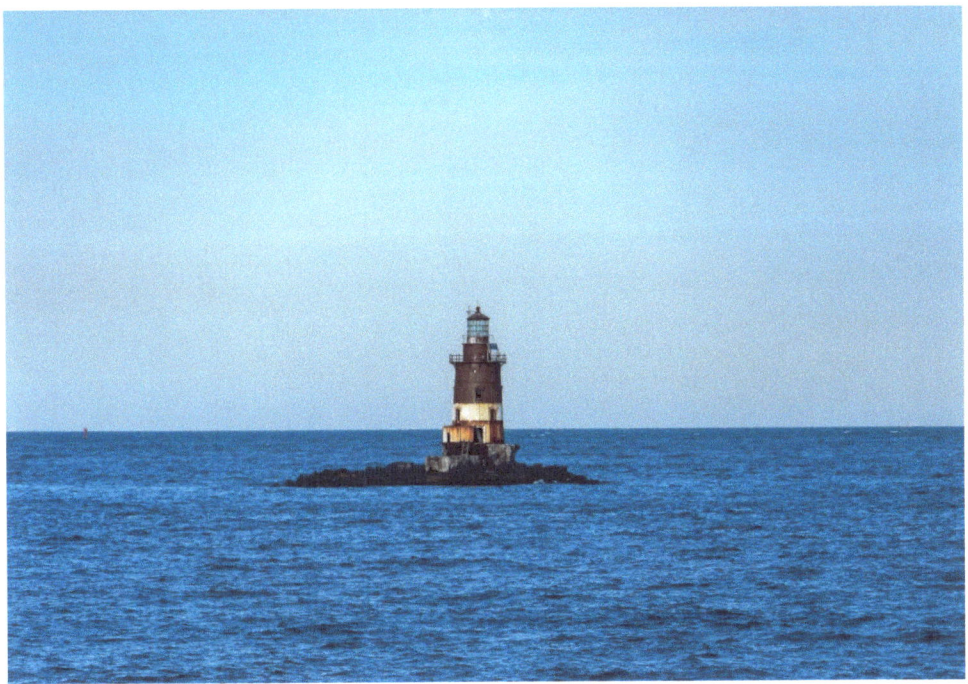

Conover Beacon

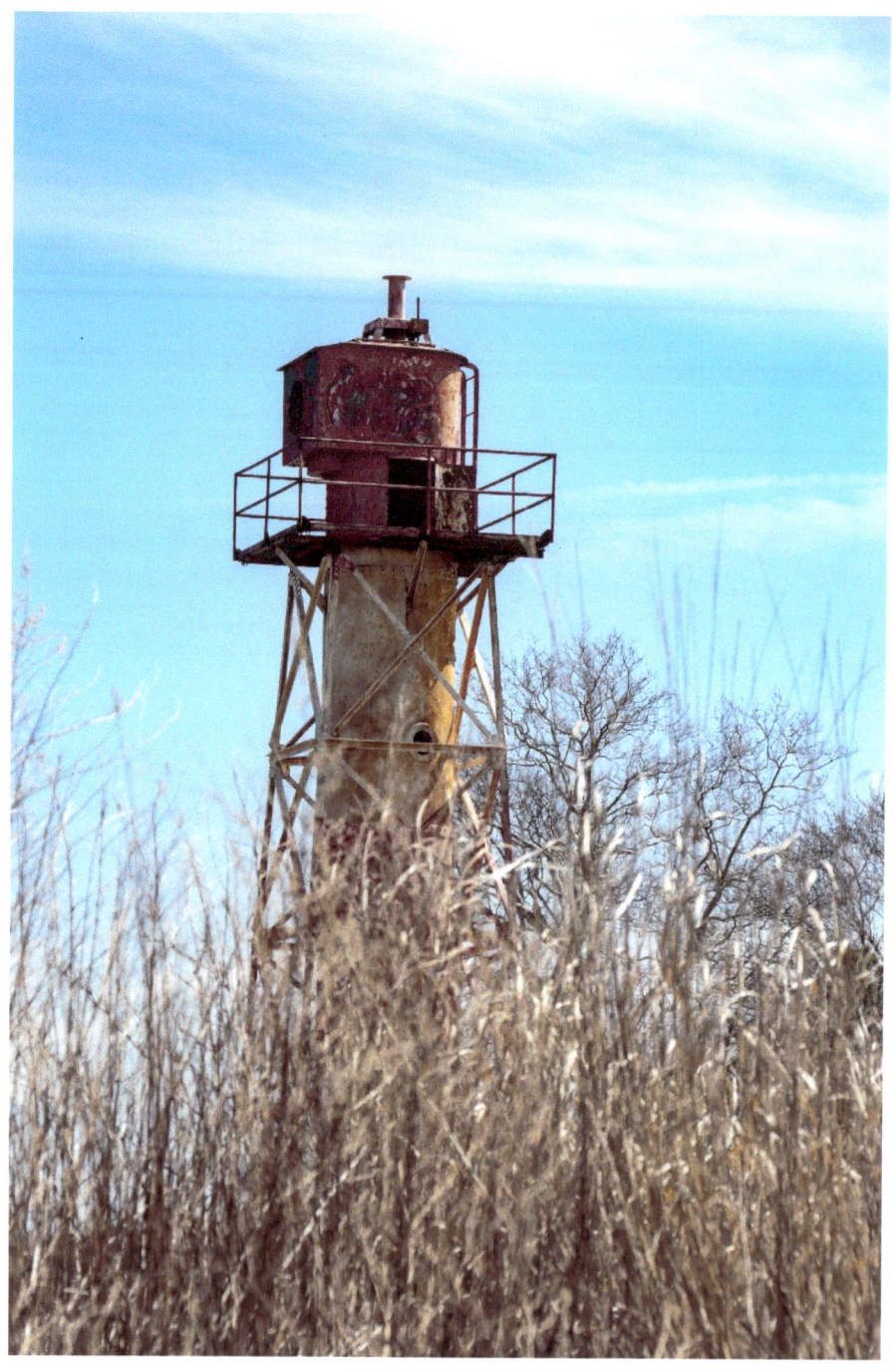

This light is located in Leonardo, New Jersey adjacent to the United States Naval Weapons Station at Earle. It is a variety of a skeleton lighthouse and the last of its particular type still standing in the United States.

The land for the original light was purchased by Congress from Rulif Conover giving the light its name, however, the location of that original site is some four miles from the current location. A wooden tower with a keeper's quarters was built on the sight in 1856 but fell into disrepair. In 1876, repairs were made to the tower and this building remained in service as navigational aid until 1923.

Construction on the current tower was completed in 1926 when it was part of the Waackaack Range serving as the front light. It was moved to its current location at Leonardo in 1941. The light is part of the Chapel Hill Range and is therefore still considered a front range light.

Range lights are configured so that when one light appears directly above another when viewed from the water, the mariner was assured that the heading would be clear of obstructions. In this case, the lights provided guidance to Chapel Hill Channel. A front range light was in front of a rear range light giving both their names.

The Coast Guard decommissioned Conover Beacon in 1957 and ownership of the property was transferred to Middletown Township in 2004. Superstorm Sandy damaged the deteriorating structure in 2012, however, a local group known as *The Friends of Conover Beacon Society* has formed to try and raise the funds necessary to restore the light and surrounding grounds.

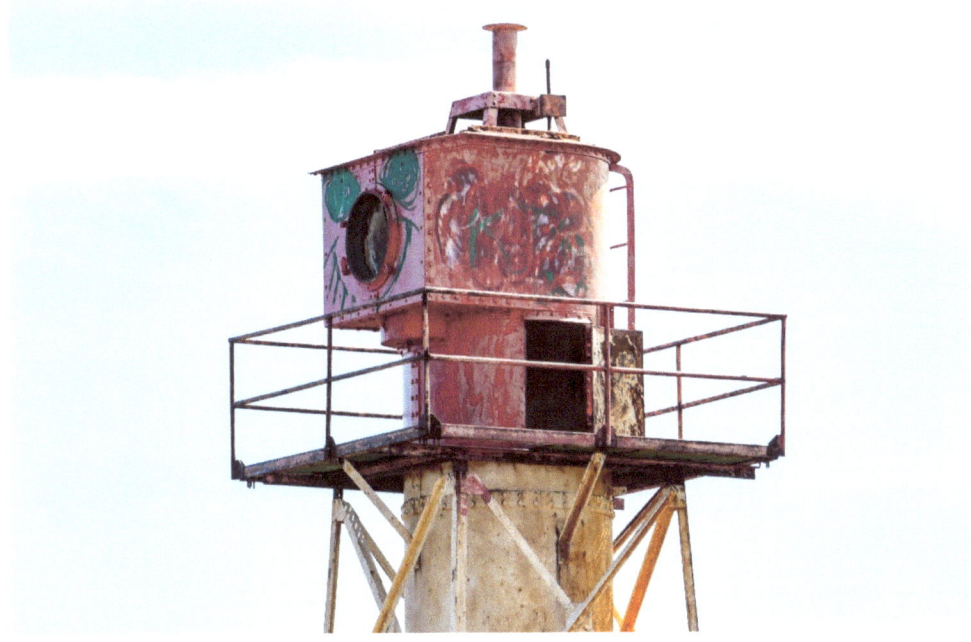

Chapel Hill Lighthouse

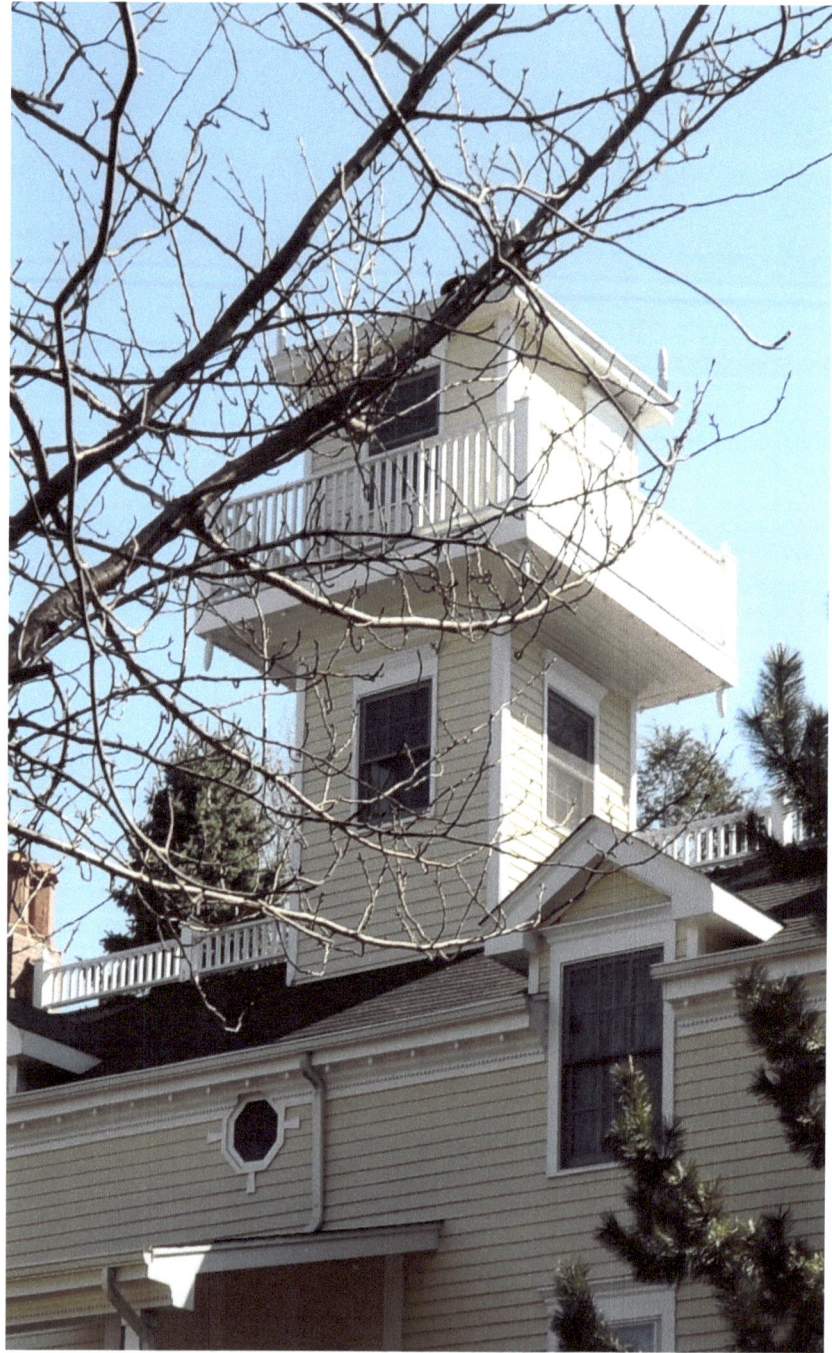

Photo courtesy of Christine Cardaci – Thelighthousehunters.com

The Chapel Hill Lighthouse was part of the Chapel Hill Range is and sometimes referred to as the Chapel Hill Rear Range light. In conjunction with the Conover Beacon, the light serves to guide mariners into Chapel Hill Channel.

The current light serving this function is a beacon on a steel pole some 200 feet north of the lighthouse called Chapel Hill. The lighthouse is now a private residence having been decommissioned as a lighthouse in 1957 and offered for sale as surplus government property.

The story goes that a wealthy businessman purchased the building for his amateur astronomer son. The building is over 150 feet above sea level putting the lantern room more than 200 feet above sea level. The site would have been ideal for stargazing.

The current building dates back to 1856 although a number of changes have been made over the years. Storms, additions, and modifications have all had an effect on the original building but the main residence and tower remain pretty much intact.

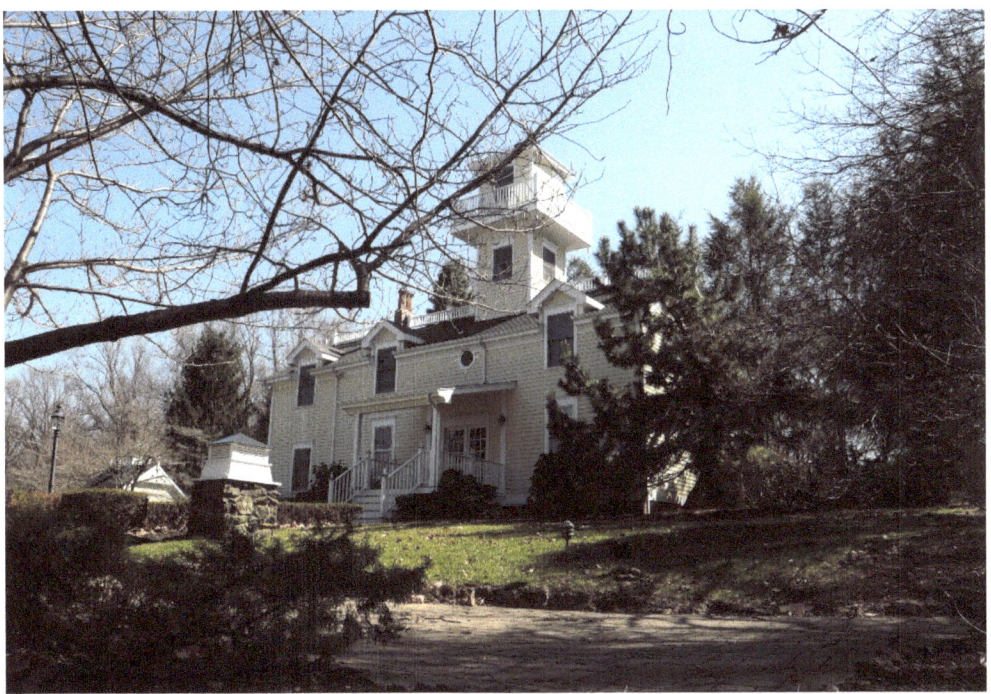

Photo courtesy of Christine Cardaci – Thelighthousehunters.com

Sandy Hook

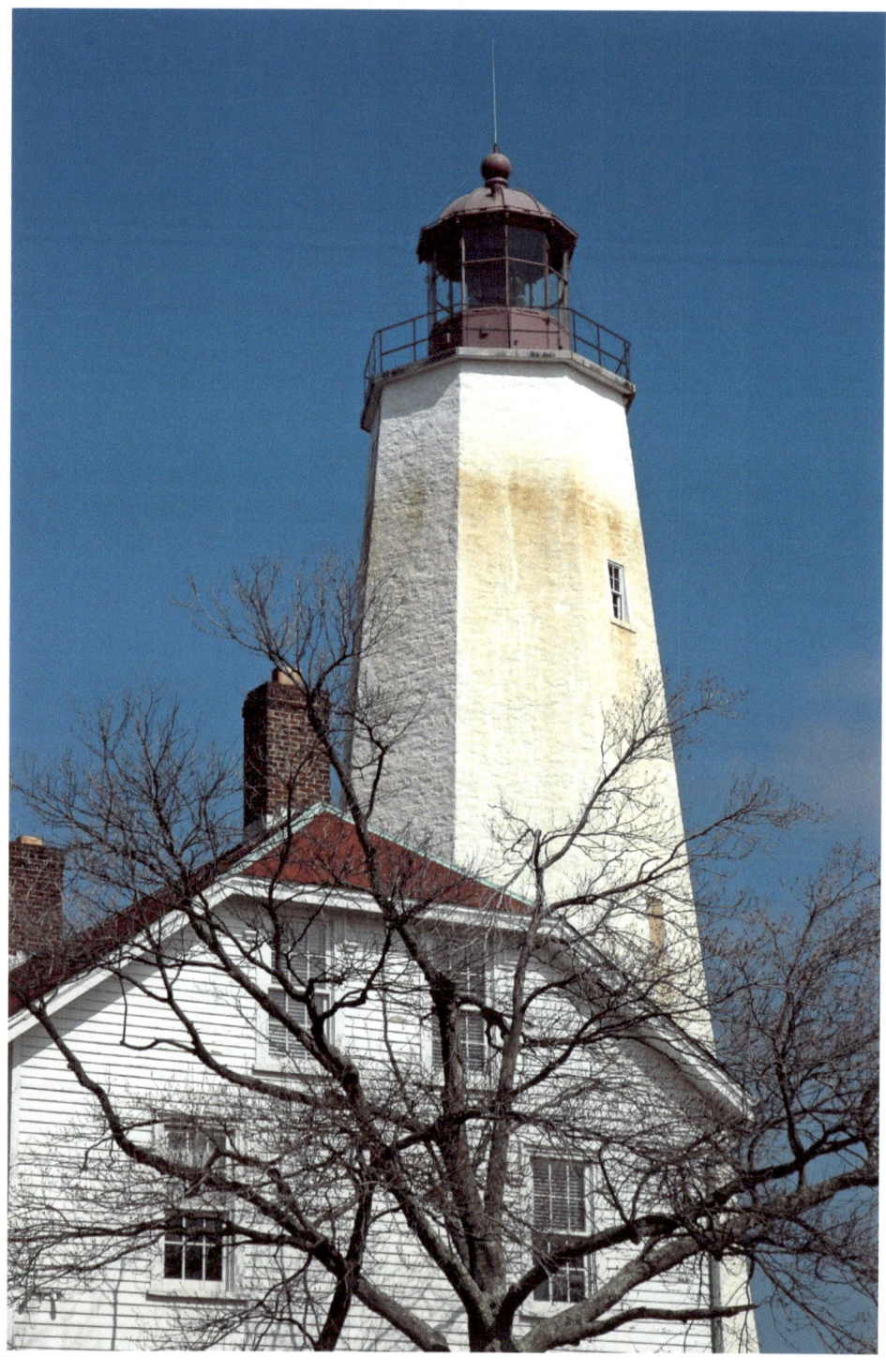

The lighthouse at Sandy Hook, New Jersey is the oldest working lighthouse in the United States. In fact, it predates the founding of the union. The New York colony authorized the construction of the lighthouse to protect the entrance to New York Harbor after shipwrecks in 1761 caused financial loss to merchants. Some 43 merchants petitioned Lieutenant Governor Caldwallader Colden, President of His Majesty's Royal Council of New York to build the lighthouse and to collect a tax from passing ships to pay for the construction. In May 1761, the Provisional Congress authorized a lottery to raise funds to acquire the land and construct the lighthouse. The lottery failed to raise the total needed for the light so additional lotteries were authorized in 1762. These added lotteries succeeded in raising the necessary funds to build the lighthouse.

First lit in 1774, the lighthouse has remained in continuous operation ever since save for brief wartime periods beginning with the Revolutionary War when operation of the light was thought to give aid to the enemy.

In addition to being the oldest working lighthouse in the United States, Sandy Hook has the distinction of being the first lighthouse in the country illuminated by an incandescent bulb.

The lighthouse is located on the grounds of Fort Hancock which is administered by the National Park Service as part of Gateway National Recreation Area. It was restored in 2000 and again in 2018 and is open to the public.

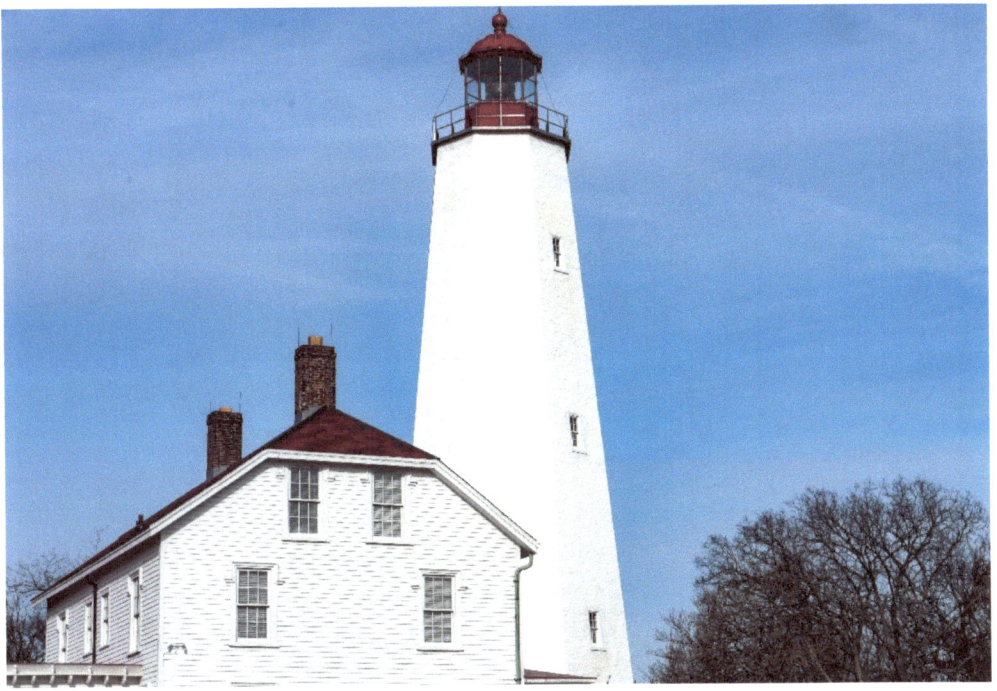

Twin Lights

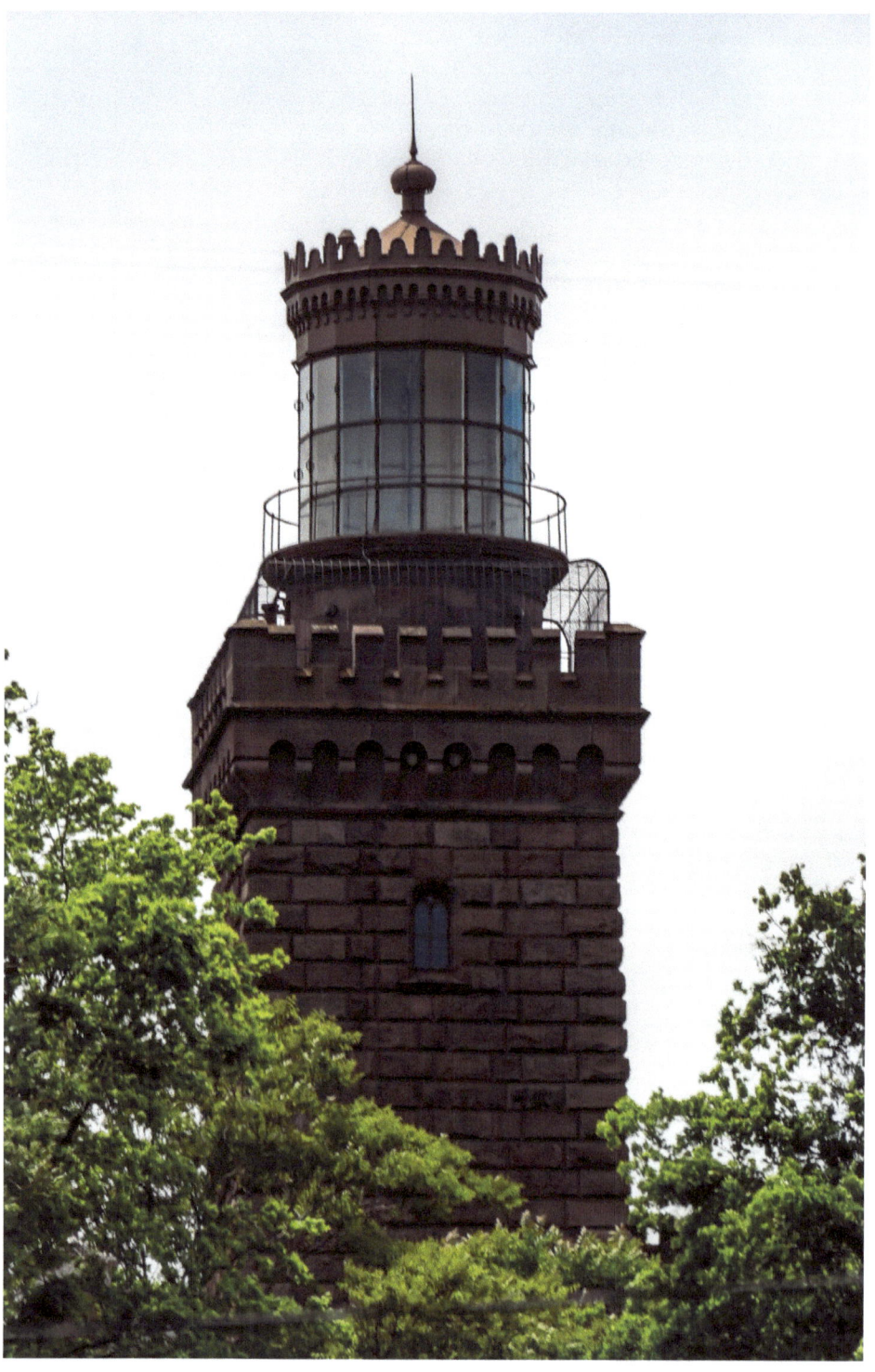

The Twin Lights are just a 12 minute drive from the lighthouse at Sandy Hook. The lights are set 200 feet above sea level in Highlands, New Jersey overlooking Highlands Reach, an extension of the Navesink River. A steep road through a residential community brings visitors to the grounds which offer sweeping views of the Navesink River, Sandy Hook, and the Atlantic Ocean.

As with the Sandy Hook light, shipping interests came together to petition Congress to build the lighthouse due to the volume of sea traffic entering New York Harbor. The shipping interests did not believe that the Sandy Hook lighthouse and the then in service Sandy Hook lightship were sufficient to protect their interests.

A lighthouse has stood on the Highlands since 1828. Although the current structure dates to 1862, it has seen its share of history.

The Twin Lights were chosen as the location for the first official recitation of the *Pledge of Allegiance*. The lights were also the location where Guglielmo Marconi received the first ever ship to shore radio communication as part of the *New York Herald*'s coverage of the America's Cup races being held off the New Jersey coast. The United States Army tested its so-called *Mystery Ray* that we now know as radar at the lights, the lights were the first in the United States that were electrically powered. And, Twin Lights were the first to use a Frensel lens.

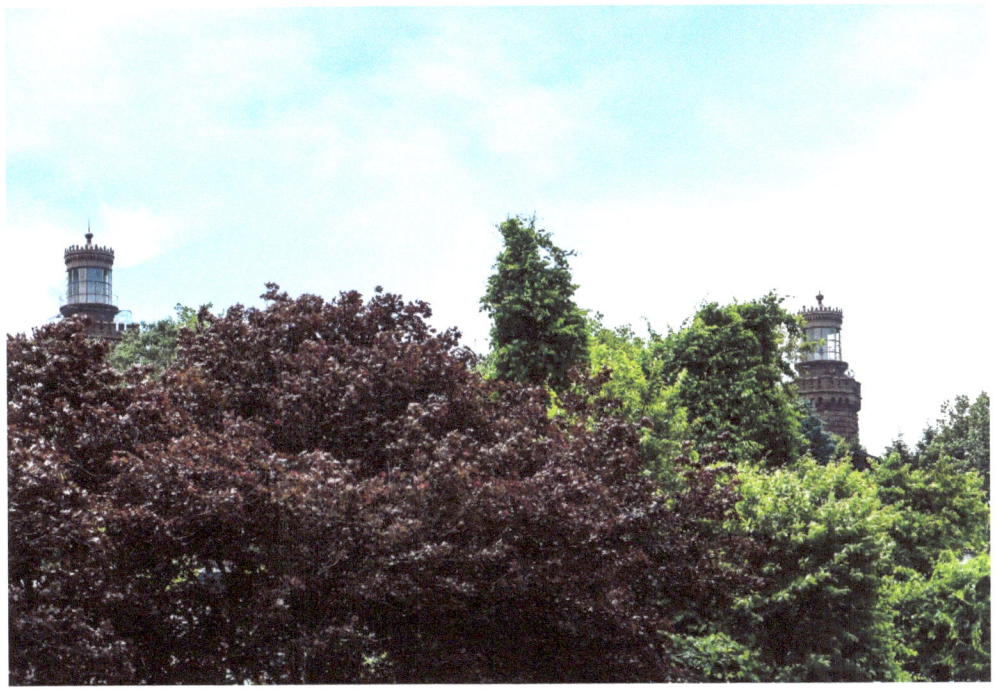

Sea Girt

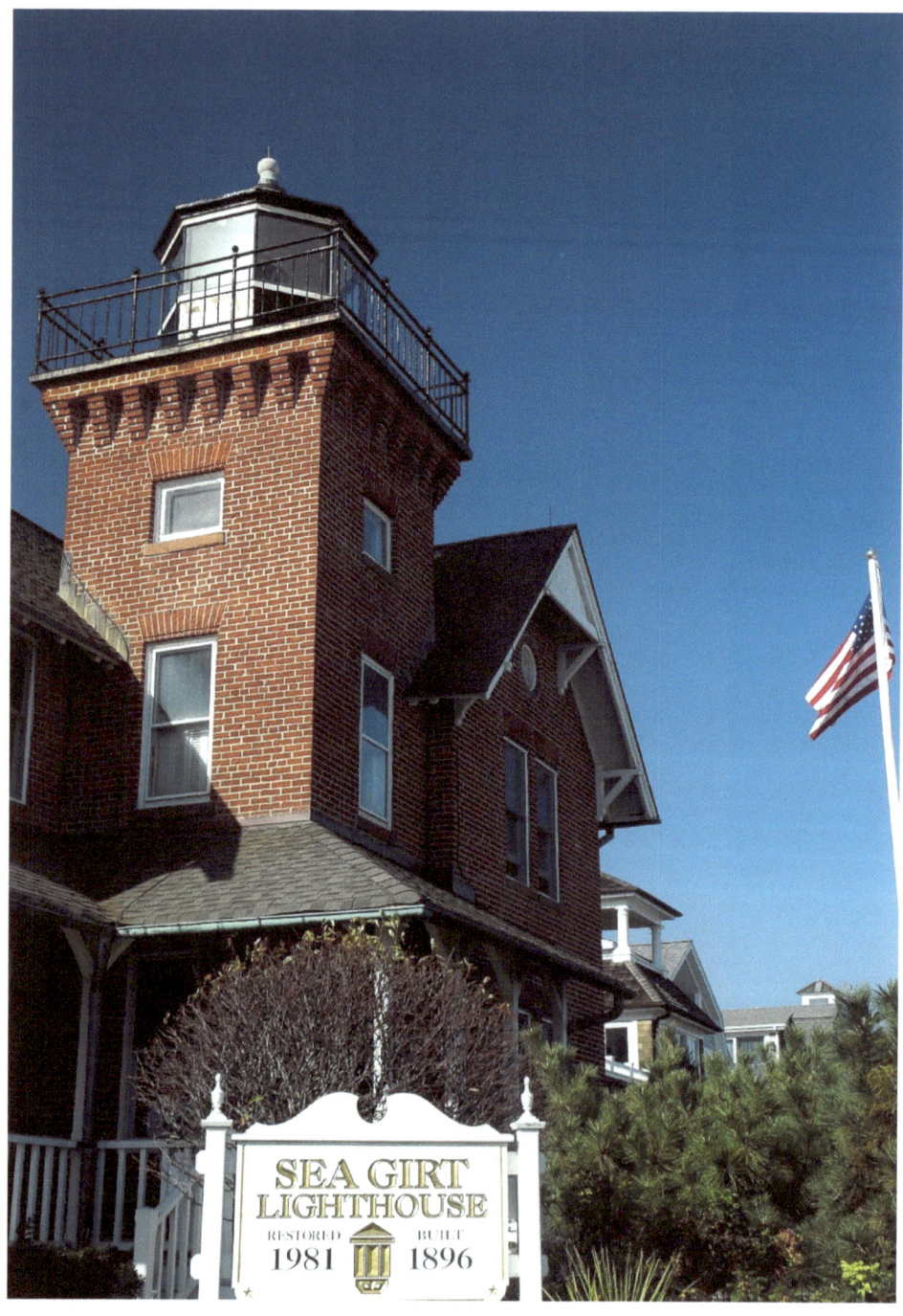

First illuminated in December of 1896, the 44 foot tower has a distinctive past.

Originally conceived to bridge a gap of more than 38 miles between the *Twin Lights* at Navesink and *Barnegat Lighthouse* in Barnegat, the lighthouse was the last live-in type lighthouse built along the United States' Atlantic coast. A live-in lighthouse integrated the keeper's quarters with the light tower. Other designs separate the structures.

In 1921, the Sea Girt Lighthouse was the first land based lighthouse to feature a radio beacon as an aid to navigation for ships at sea. In conjunction with transmitters placed on lightships *Fire Island* and *Ambrose*, mariners could accurately establish their position, even in bad weather through a process known as triangulation.

The lighthouse helped guide survivors of the deadly *Morro Castle* ship fire to safety during a storm that beached the ship in 1934. In addition to guiding the survivors to shore, the lighthouse served as a first aid station during the disaster.

After automation and ultimate decommissioning of the lighthouse, it was, at varying times, a library, a meeting hall, and a recreation center. The lighthouse was restored in the early 1980s and now serves as a museum and tourist attraction reminding visitors of its role in history and in tragedy.

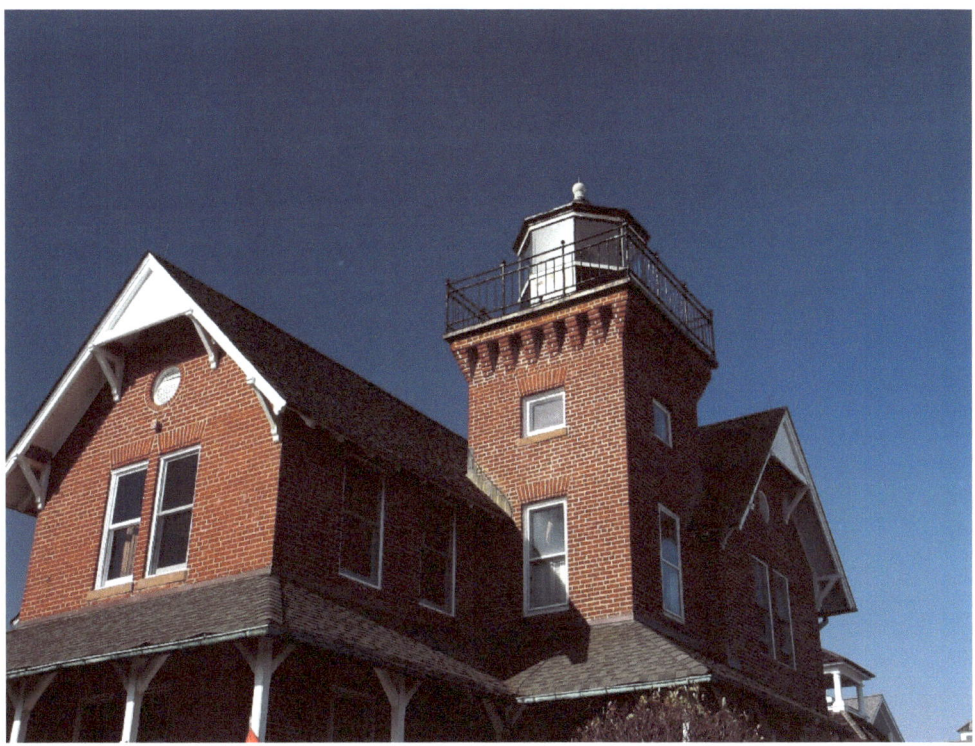

Barnegat Light

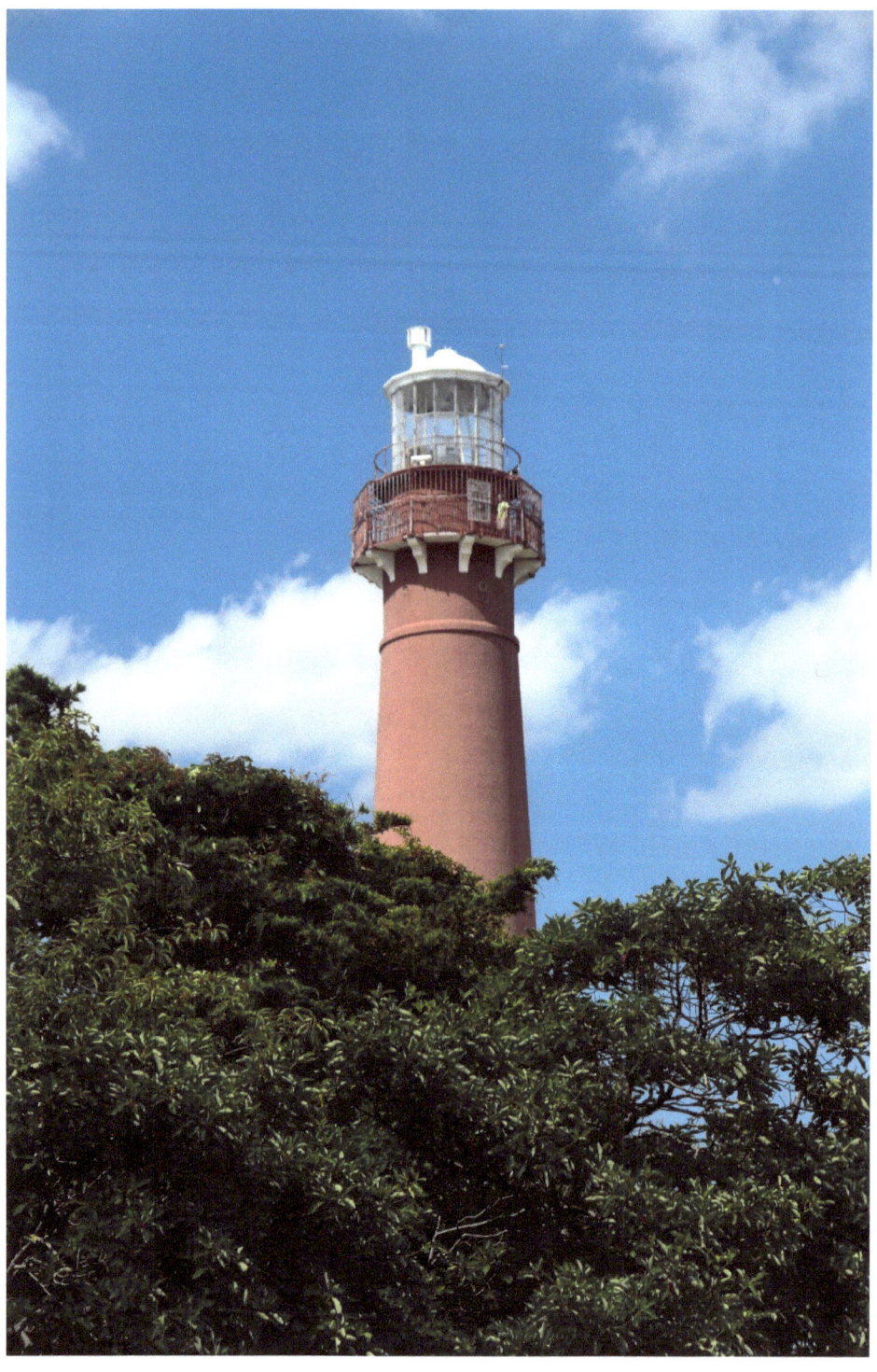

Affectionately known as *Old Barney*, this lighthouse sits at the northern end of Long Beach Island providing guidance for mariners entering Barnegat Inlet. .A light has stood in this area since 1834 but the current building dates to 1859. George G. Meade of the United States Army designed the lighthouse. Meade would later gain notoriety as a Major General for the union defeating Robert E. Lee at Gettysburg during the American Civil War.

The tower is 169 feet tall putting the light itself more than 170 feet above sea level.

The lighthouse was made operational once again in 2009 after a hiatus of more than 60 years with a VRB-25 optical system that was purchased by the *Friends of Barnegat Lighthouse*, a local non-profit community group. The current system is visible at sea for 22 nautical miles. A foghorn system is also installed at the end of the jetty guarding the inlet.

The lighthouse is so important to the local area that in 1948 the town of *Barnegat City* renamed itself *Barnegat Light*, a name that it retains to this day.

Barnegat Lighthouse is on the grounds of *Barnegat Lighthouse State Park*. Visitors can climb to the top of the lighthouse for spectacular views of the Atlantic Ocean, Barnegat Bay, and the surrounding communities. They can also walk a maritime trail and visit a museum located a short distance away. The grounds of the state park are also an important part of the Atlantic Flyway for migrating birds. Endangered species nest on the park grounds and many bird species can be observed during the annual spring and fall migrations.

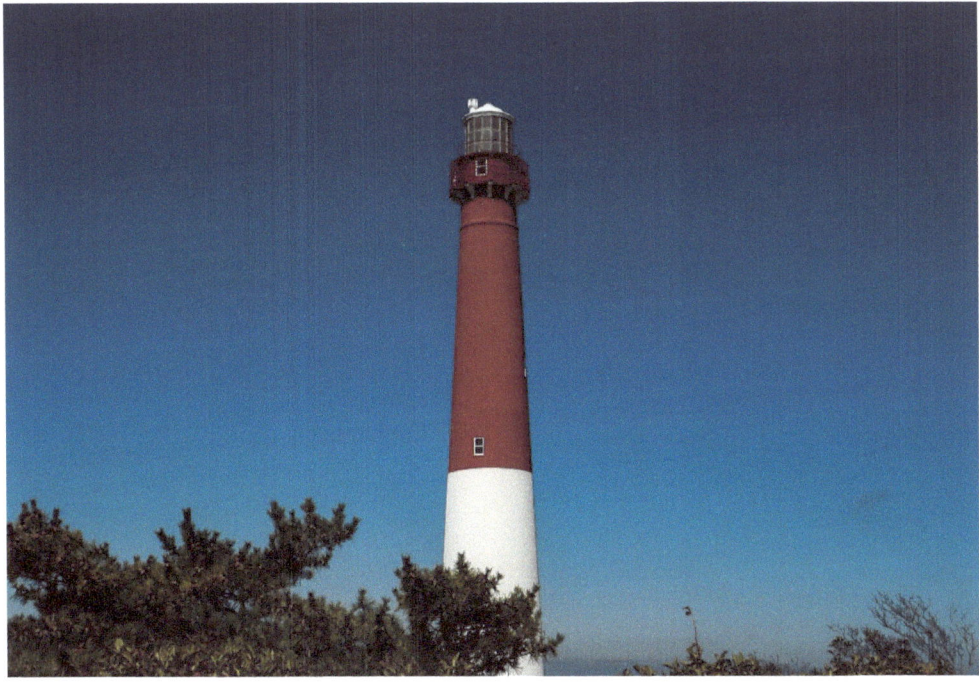

Tucker's Island Light

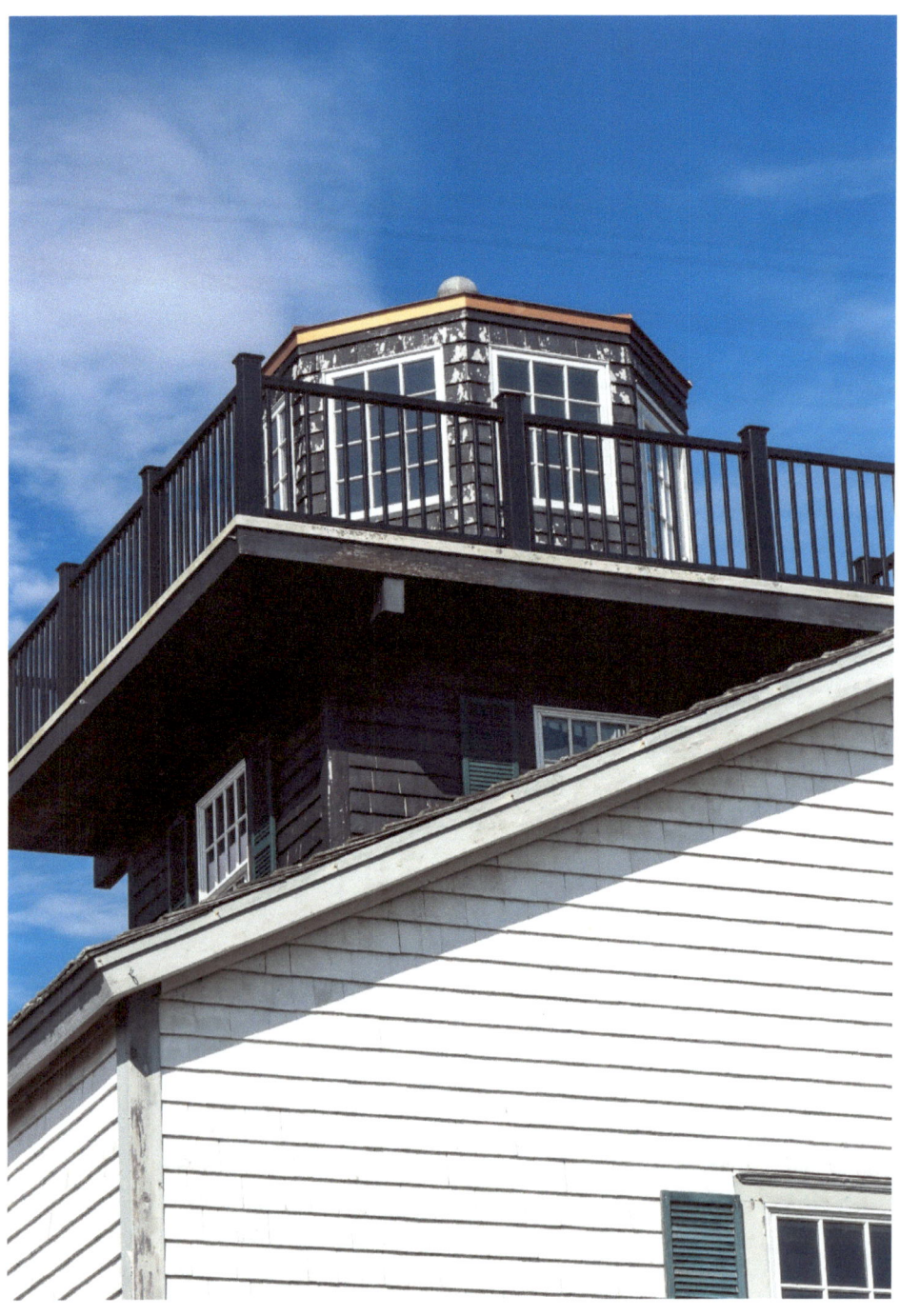

The lighthouse located in Tuckerton is a replica of the lighthouse once located on Tucker's Island that protected Little Egg Harbor. A 1920 storm destroyed the original lighthouse. The current building is part of Tuckerton Seaport and dates back to the year 2000.

Tuckerton Seaport is operated by *Tuckerton Seaport Baymen's Museum*. The mission of the organization is to *preserve, present and interpret the rich maritime history, artistry, heritage and environment of the Jersey shore and the unique contributions of its baymen*. It is a working museum and village with the lighthouse as its centerpiece.

Although a replica, many visitors believe the lighthouse is authentic. The New Jersey Lighthouse Society even includes a listing for Tucker's Island Light. As a designated Port of Entry into the United States it does have historic significance because it received this designation early in US history. Its role in history is why the light is still considered one of the Lighthouses of New Jersey.

On display at the museum is an original Fresnel lens from Brandywine Shoal lighthouse in Delaware Bay. Although on display, it is not in the lantern room at the top of the tower. Efforts to return the lens to its original location have so far been unsuccessful.

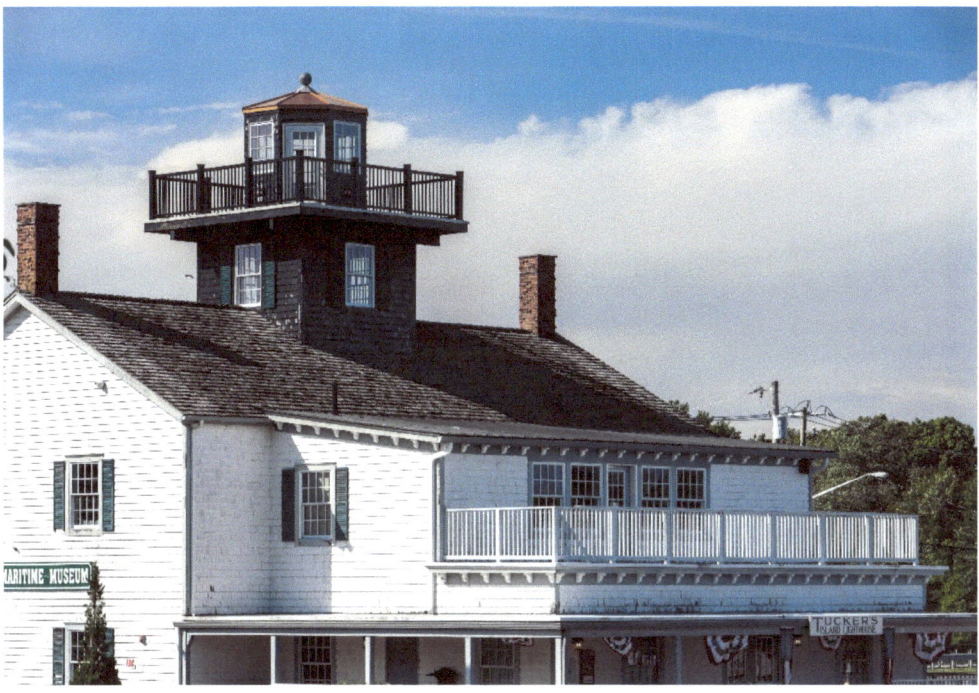

Hereford Inlet lighthouse

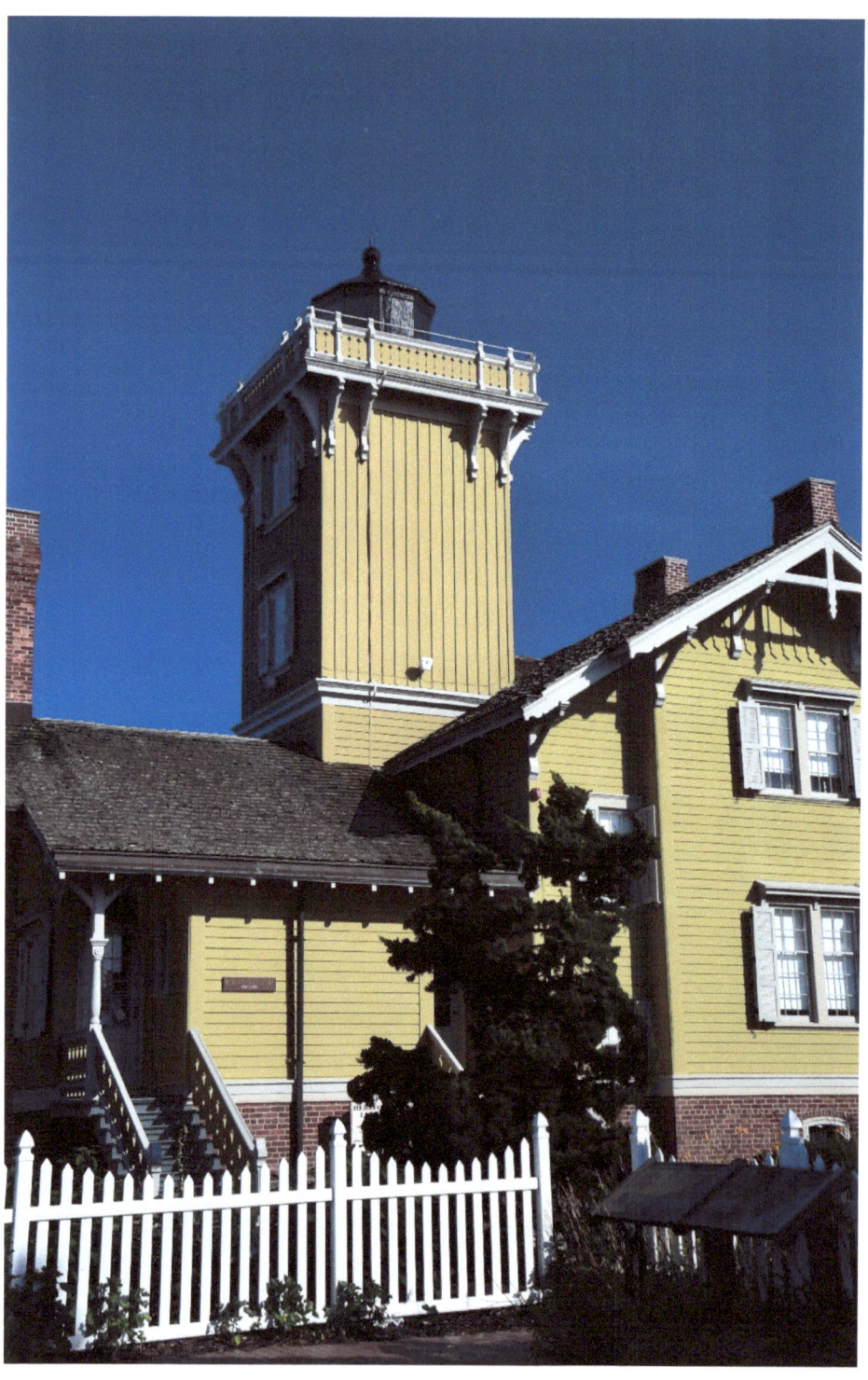

A diminutive lighthouse, the Hereford Inlet Lighthouse stands only 50 feet tall.

The lighthouse is officially located in North Wildwood but locals still know the area as Anglesea a name that it once had. Congress appropriated the funds to build the lighthouse in 1872 and the construction was complete by 1874. The light was added to an existing lifesaving station.

The original lighthouse survived storms and fires but had badly deteriorated from the time it was first closed in the 1960s until the 1980s when the property was transferred to the town of North Wildwood. A maritime unit of the New Jersey State occupies the adjacent remains of the lifesaving station but the original lighthouse was placed into private hands.

The *Friends of Hereford Inlet Lighthouse* oversaw a restoration of the lighthouse in the 1980s but as of 2018, they are no longer involved with managing or maintaining the lighthouse. Control of the property has been transferred to the City of North Wildwood causing a local controversy. Long-time volunteers at the lighthouse are concerned about its future.

The current light was once the replacement light that stood on a separate tower. It has been in operation in the original lighthouse since being moved there in 1986.

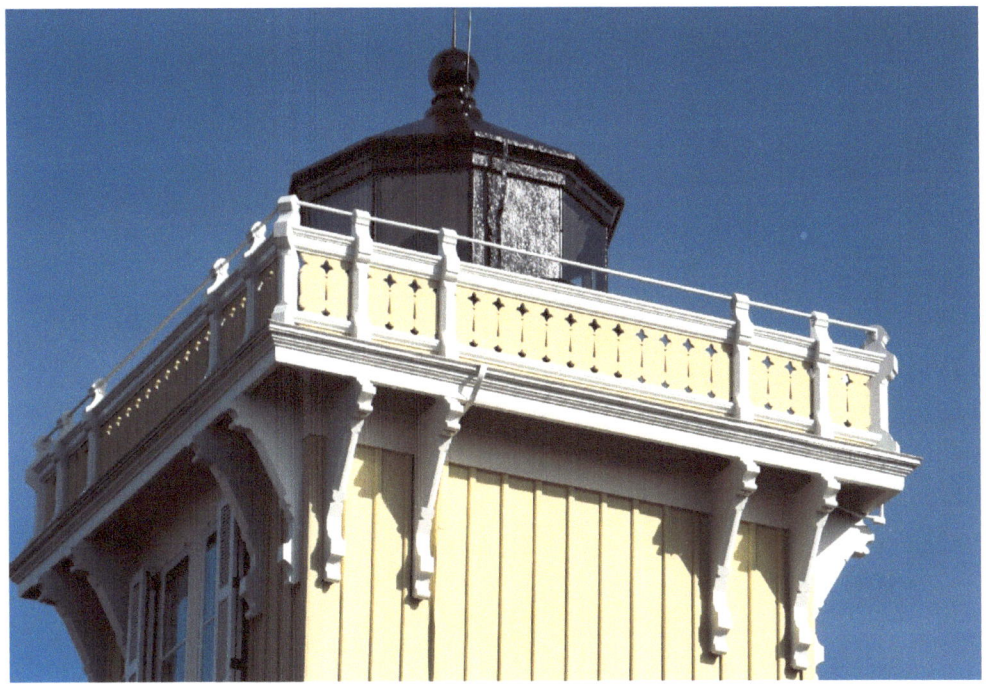

Absecon Lighthouse

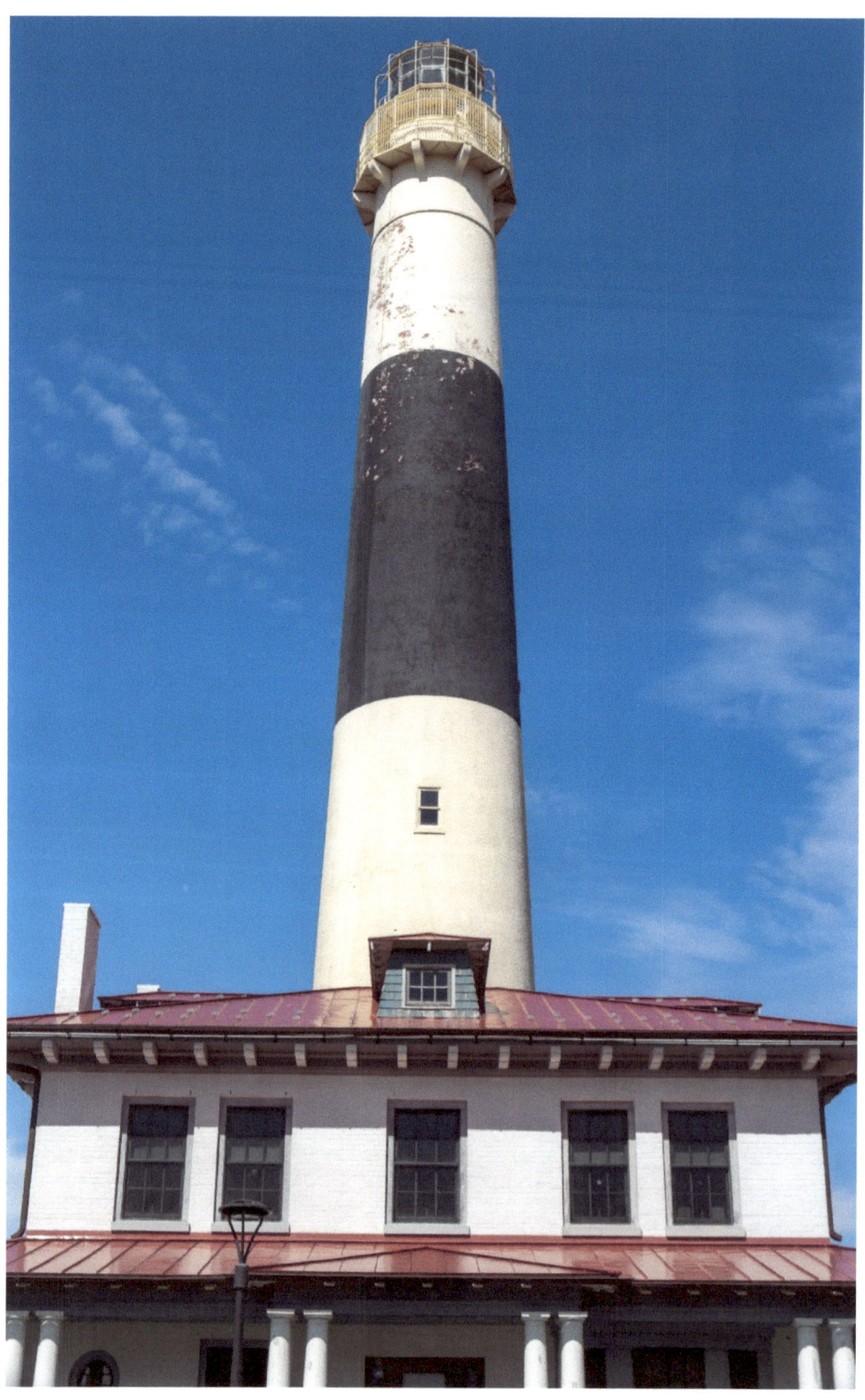

The Absecon lighthouse is located in Atlantic City, New Jersey. Today it is lost among the mega casino hotels that populate the area even though the lighthouse stands 171 feet tall making it the tallest lighthouse in the Garden State and third tallest in the United States.

Congress appropriated money for the acquisition of land in 1854 after a series of notable shipwrecks. The tipping point came when the ship *Powhattan*, arriving from Europe, wrecked with a large number of immigrants on board. Somewhere between 200 and 350 people are known to have lost their lives in the wreck thereby spurring lawmakers to act.

Construction began in 1856 with George G. Meade of the United States Army as part of the engineering team. The first illumination was in 1857 and the light was extinguished in 1933 and ownership transferred to the city of Atlantic City.

Today Absecon Lighthouse retains its original first-order Fresnel lens. In fact, it is the only lighthouse in New Jersey that has its first-order lens still in its original location. The lighthouse has been recently restored to include a replica of the keeper's home.

The paint scheme today reflects the 1948 livery. The light has been painted and repainted several times. At its first lighting, the lighthouse was unpainted natural brick.

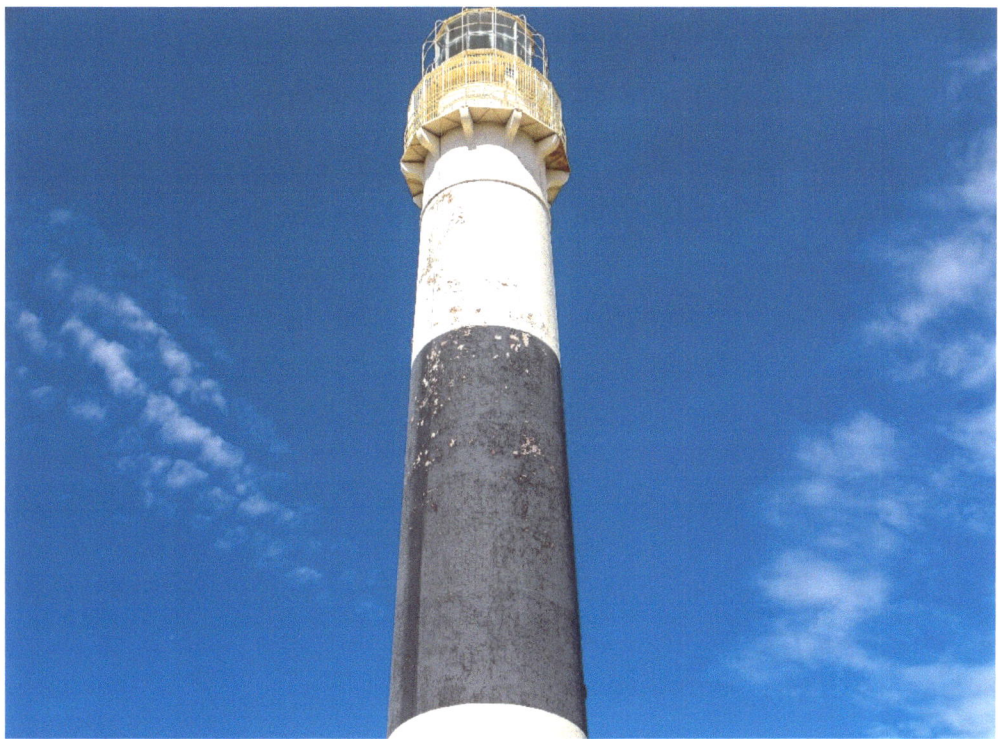

Cape May

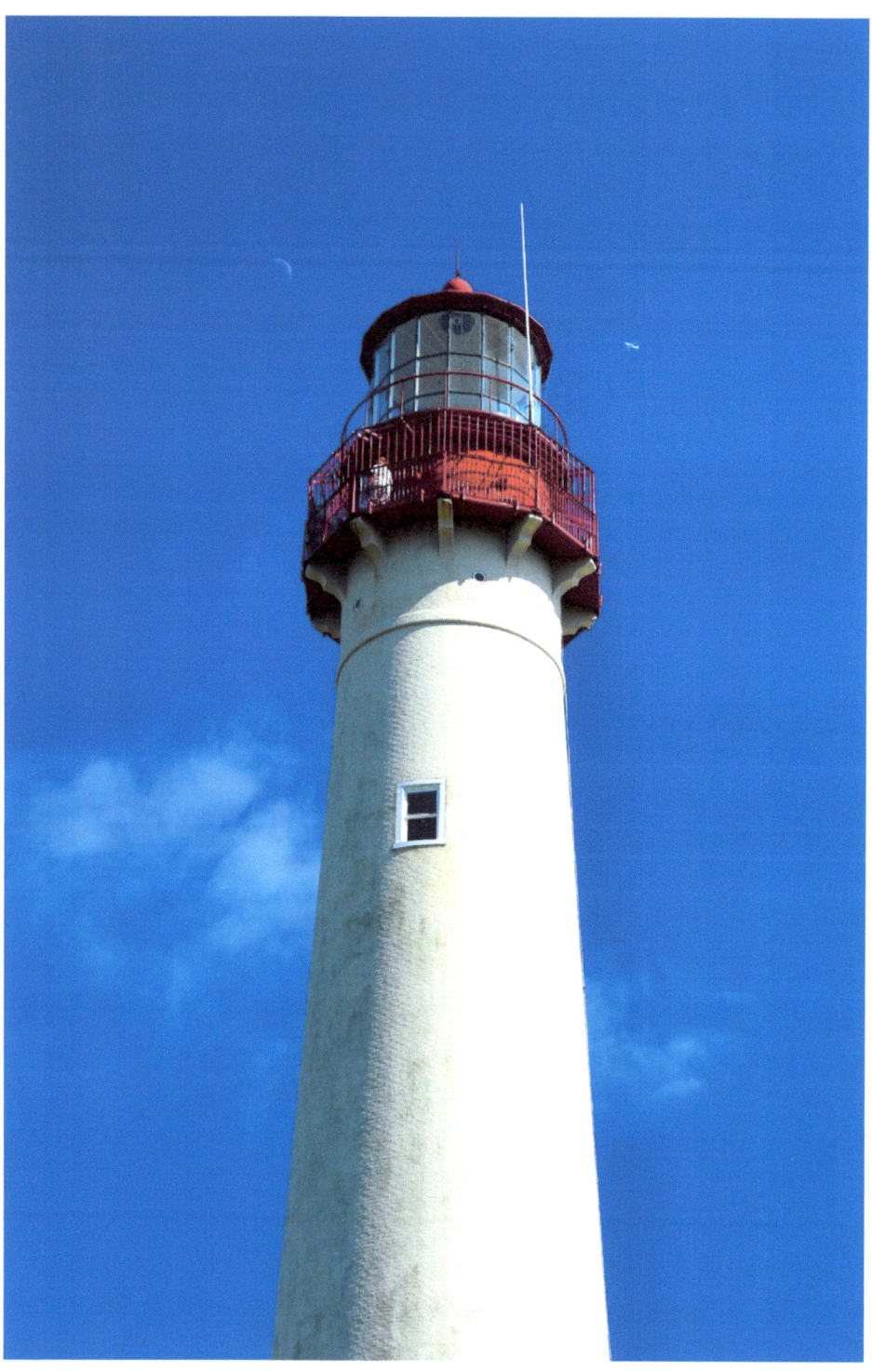

The lighthouse at Cape May is the southernmost lighthouse in New Jersey. Located within *Cape May Point State Park*, the lighthouse is actually further south than Baltimore, MD and just about as far south as Washington DC.

The light continues to operate today having first been illuminated in 1859. The current lighthouse is the third to mark the southern end of New Jersey with the locations of the prior two now under water.

The light was fully automated in 1946 and was transferred from United States Coast Guard ownership to the State of New Jersey in 1992. The state leases the property to the Mid-Atlantic Center for Arts & Humanities an organization that runs the museum and interpretative center for the lighthouse.

The lighthouse is over 157 feet tall making it is the third tallest lighthouse in New Jersey behind Absecon Light (171 feet) and Barnegat Light (163 feet).

Operating today with a VRB-25 optical system, the light originally boasted a first-order Fresnel Lens. The light can be seen for 24 miles.

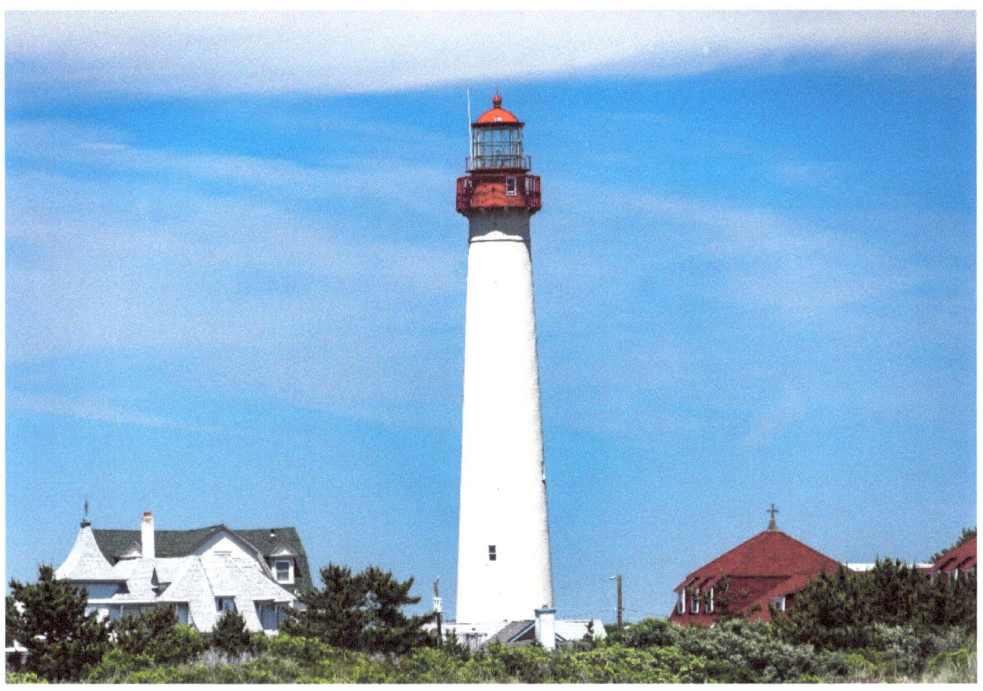

Brandywine Shoal

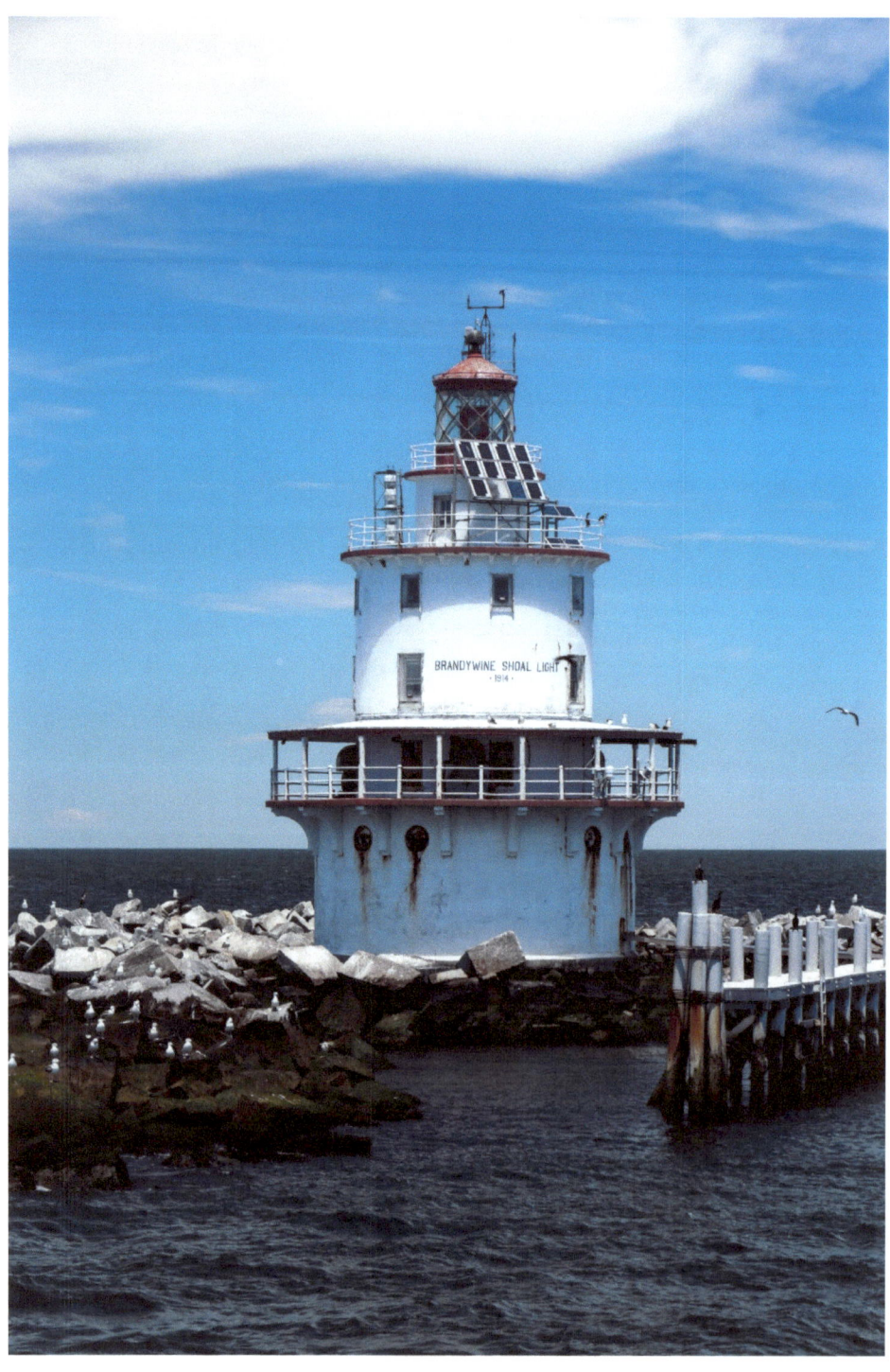

This lighthouse location, 8.8 miles WNW of Cape May, New Jersey, presents some significant history of lighthouses in the United States. Three lighthouses and a lightship have served the area.

The first lighthouse was intended to replace a deteriorating lightship on the sight. This effort did not last a full year as storms and heavy seas destroyed the building. The second lighthouse on the site was a screw-pile lighthouse, the first in the United States.

A screw-pile lighthouse is a building constructed on pilings that are screwed into the sea bed. George G. Meade was involved in the design of this lighthouse, installation, and modifications to the lighthouse and it was first lit in 1850. In 1851, a third-order Fresnel lens was added to the light, only the third installation in the United States as The Lighthouse Board was testing the technology. This light survived until the early 20th Century when concerns over corrosion of the wood pilings caused the replacement light to be built.

The third lighthouse to mark the spot is the sparkplug type lighthouse that you see today. This light, built in 1914, features a concrete superstructure on a cast-iron base. The original third-order lens from the second lighthouse was used in the third but has since been placed in the Tuckerton Seaport. The light was automated in 1974 having been the last of the Delaware Bay lighthouses to be manned.

The light operates today as a continuing aid to navigation. The United States General Services Administration made the light available to eligible entities as part of the National Historic Lighthouse Preservation Act. A local tour operator, Cape May Whale Watchers, formed a non-profit to obtain the light and raise funds for its preservation.

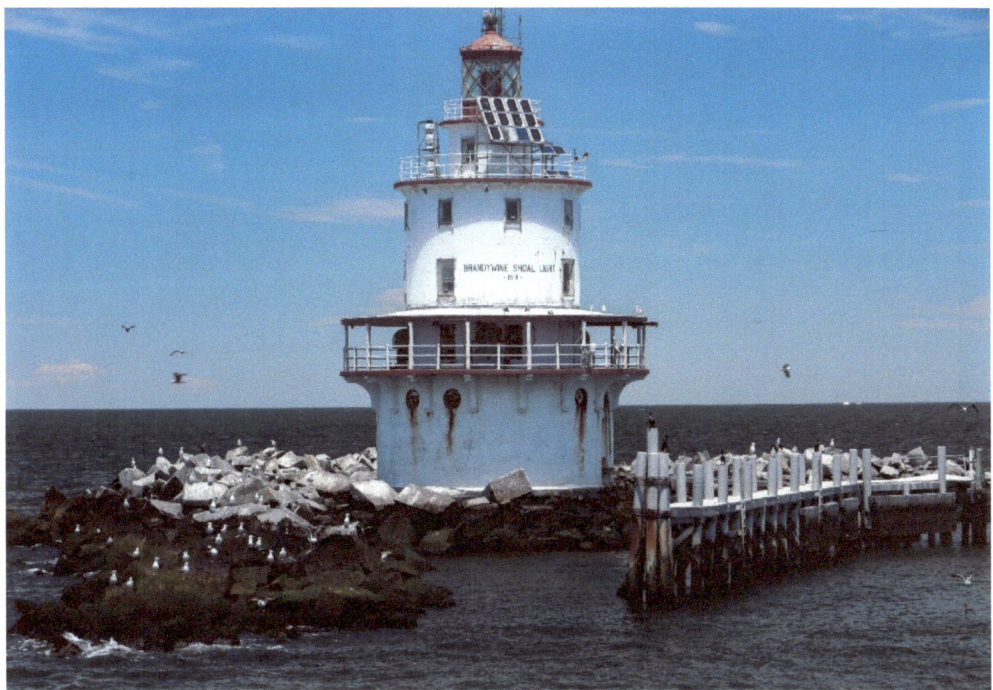

East Point Lighthouse

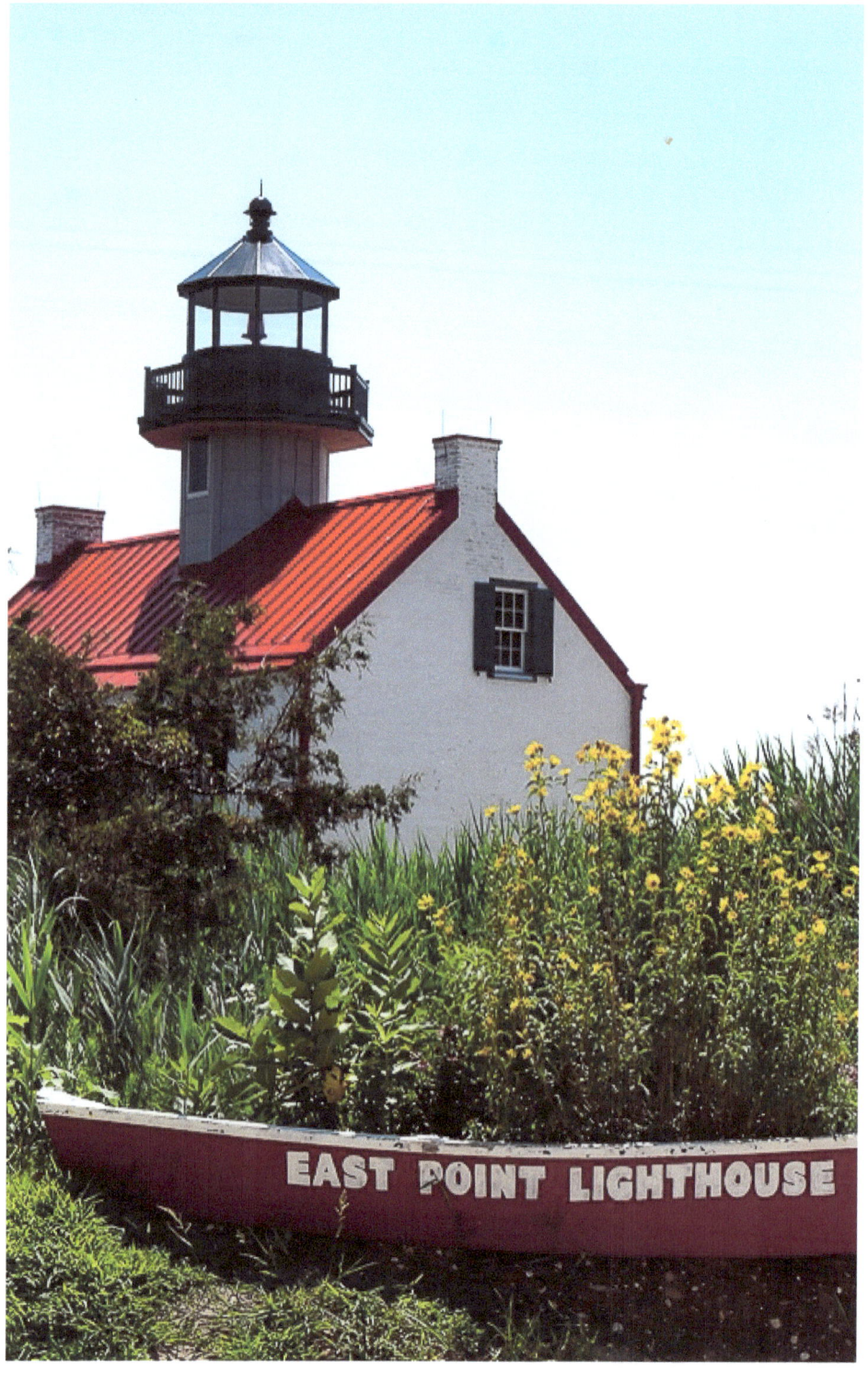

On Delaware Bay, this lighthouse has roots in range lights placed along the coast. The Lighthouse Board, at the time, recommended these lights due to the number of shipwrecks occurring at the mouth of the Maurice River. In fact, the lighthouse was originally named the Maurice River Lighthouse. The current lighthouse is the second oldest in New Jersey opening in 1849.

The light remained in operation until the outbreak of World War II when it was turned off for reasons of national security. After the war, the Coast Guard deemed the light to be unnecessary and the lighthouse was decommissioned. In 1955, the government declared the building and land surplus and put them up for auction.

The auction resulted in a high bid from a construction company, however, the State of New Jersey cried foul for the fact that it had not been offered the property first as required by regulations. Reversing the results of the sale, the property was eventually deeded to New Jersey.

The building deteriorated over time and local residents took up the cause of possible restoration of the lighthouse. In 1971, the *Maurice River Historical Society* was formed and part of its mission was to raise money to restore the lighthouse. Before this mission could be fulfilled, a fire heavily damaged the building. This delayed progress on the restoration, however, the society was able to begin the project with grant money and in 1980 the Coast Guard relit the light.

Restoration work continued as money was available and in 2017, the work was substantially done. The lighthouse was rededicated at that time.

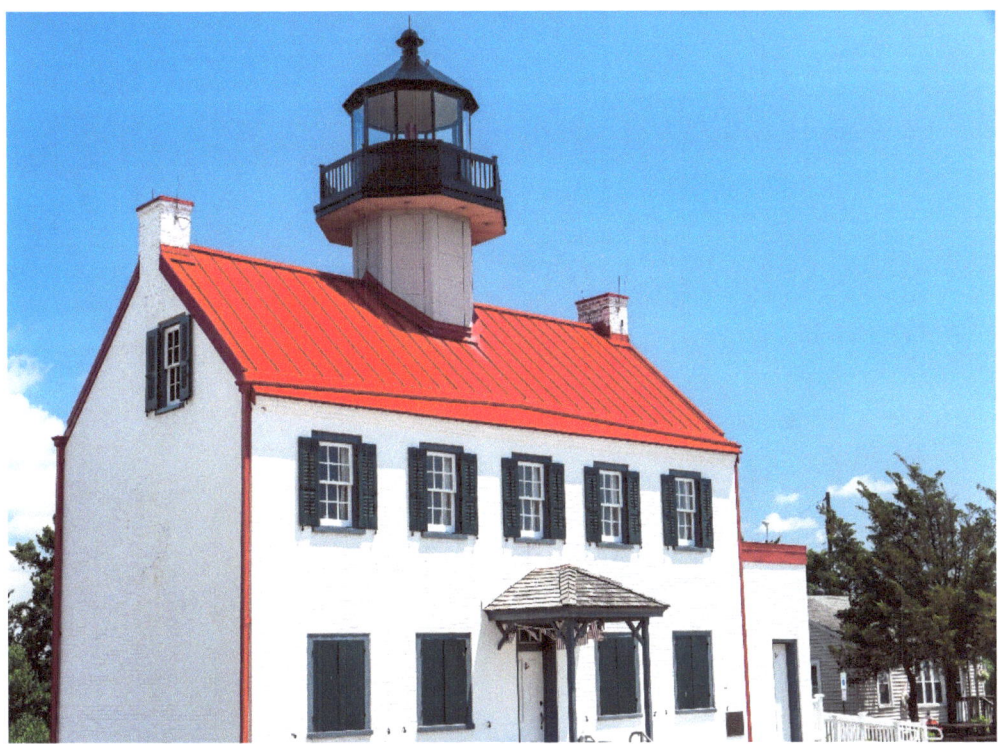

Miah Maull

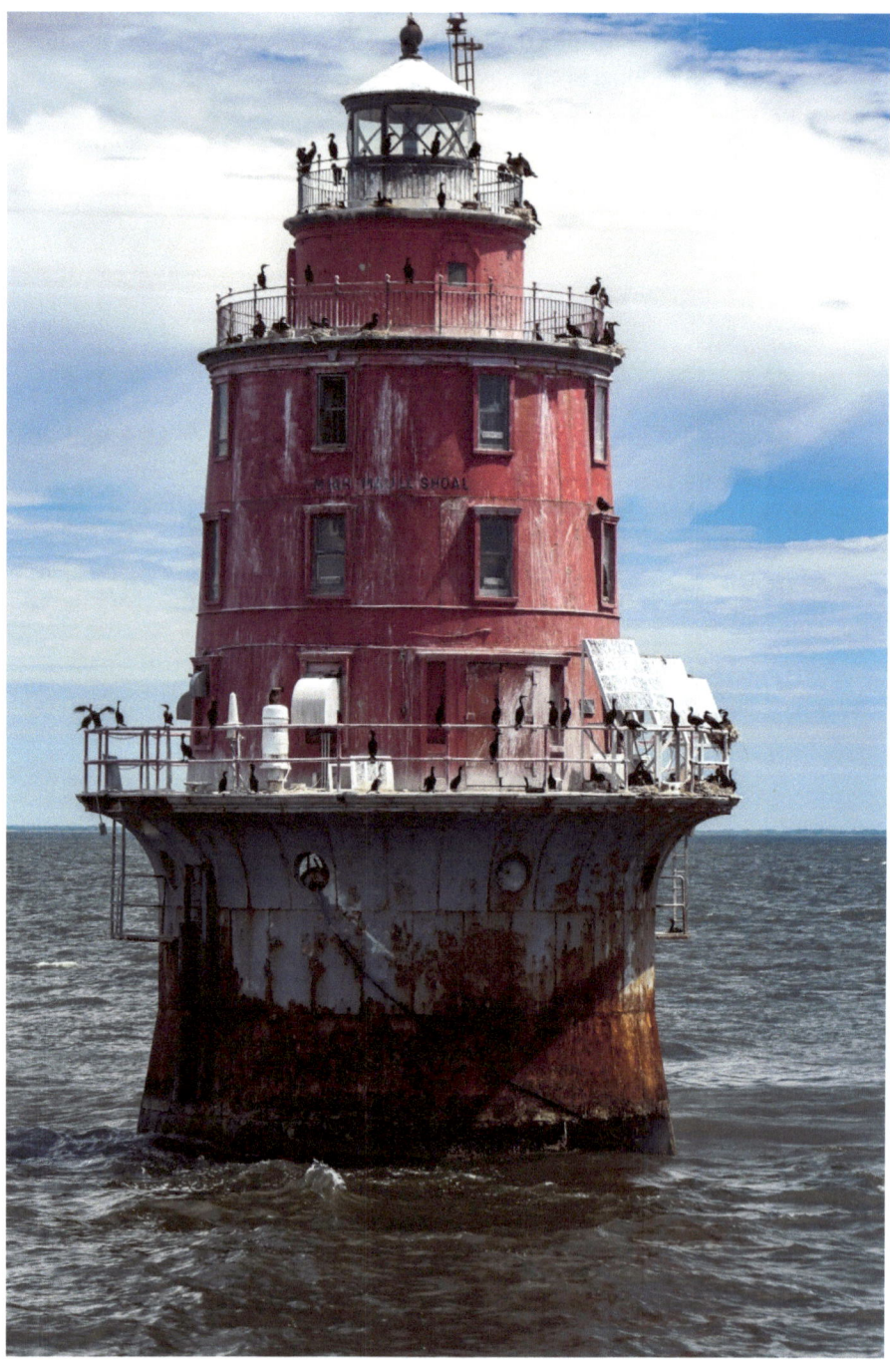

This sparkplug type lighthouse marks Miah Maull Shoal in Delaware Bay. Named after Nehemiah Maull, the shoal is the site of numerous shipwrecks. Maull was a Delaware River pilot who ironically drowned when the vessel in which he was just a passenger grounded on a shoal. In honor of his long service on Delaware Bay, the shoal that the current lighthouse guards was named in his honor.

Although Maull worked on Delaware Bay in the 18th Century, his namesake lighthouse was not built until the 20th Century. Construction was authorized in 1904 but it wasn't until 1909 that a temporary light became operational.

The permanent light was lit in 1913 with a temporary fog warning bell installed. The lighthouse has had multiple lenses over its lifetime. The original rotating lens was replaced with a US made fourth-order Fresnel lens that remained in service until 1999. This light was visible for 15 miles. The station was manned until 1973 when the Coast Guard automated the light.

The photo shows no covering over the walkway at the base of the light; however, the original installation had a metal cover. This was removed when it was found to be beyond repair.

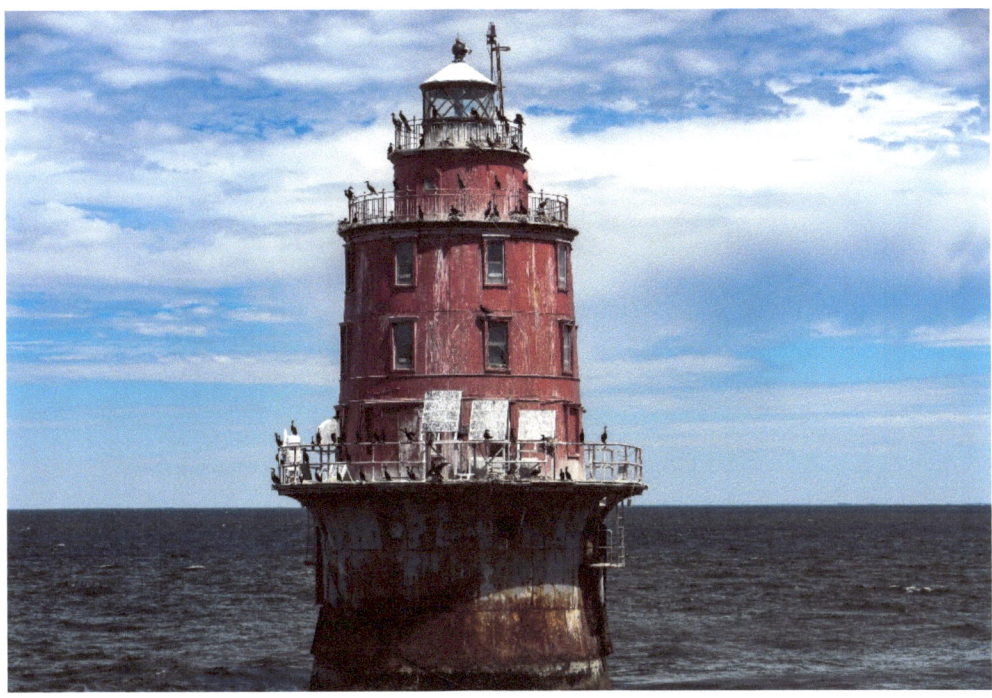

Elbow of Cross Ledge

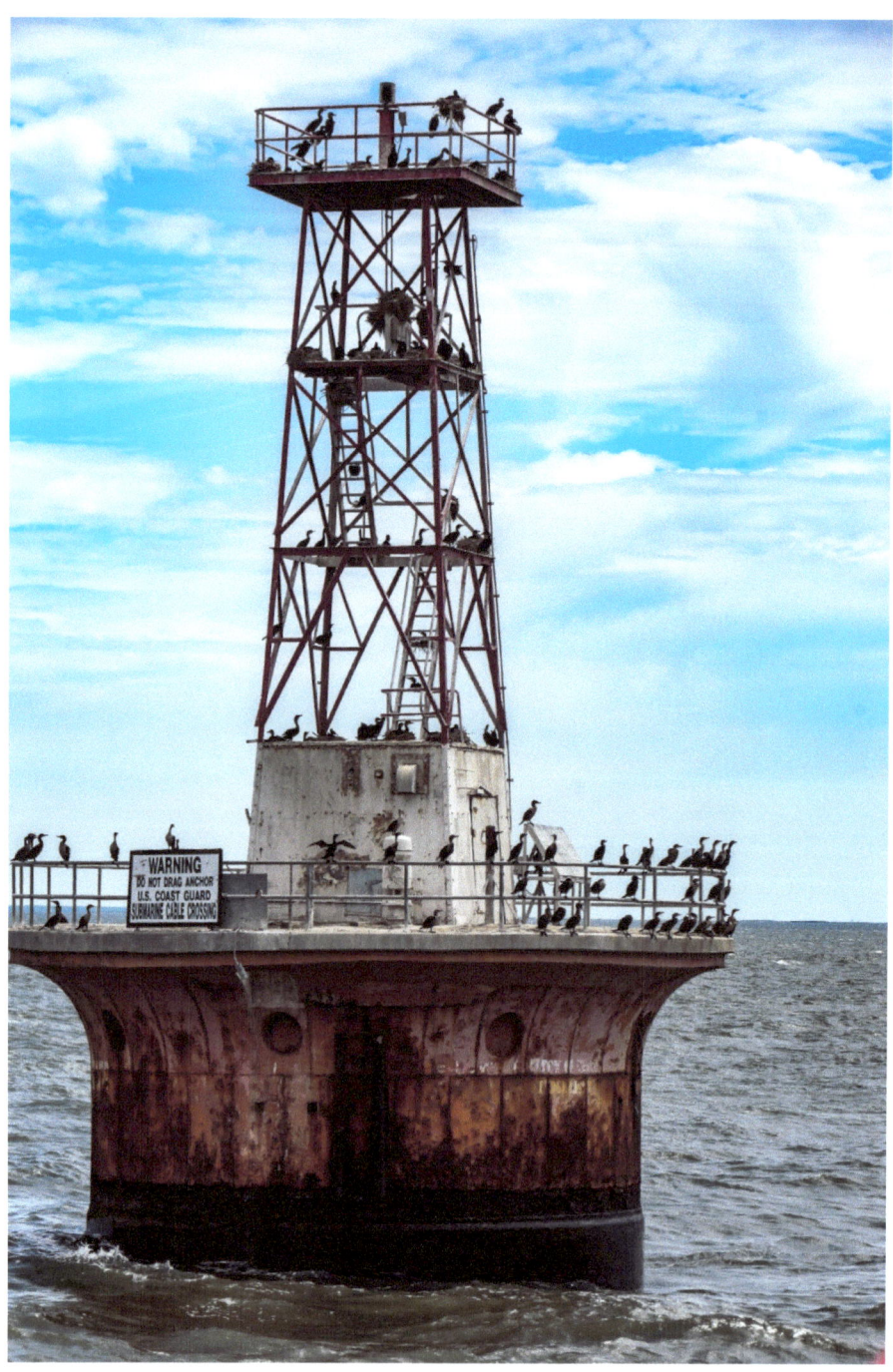

Another unusual name. This Skeleton Type lighthouse replaced an all brick structure in 1953 after the original 1910 lighthouse was destroyed when a ship collided with it.

The interesting name comes from a ledge that forms the shoal marked by the light and the *elbow* in that ledge.

The original light was a fourth-order Fresnel lens manufactured by an American company, Barbier, Bernard, and Turenne. A fog bell was installed and operating when the station was first lit.

In 1932, electricity came to the station and an air horn replaced the fog bell.

Storms and near collisions where commonplace at the lighthouse so much so that the *Philadelphia Evening Bulletin* quoted a United States Coast Guard officer as saying that the crew of the lighthouse often slept with their life jackets on ready to make a quick exit should the lighthouse be struck by a passing ship.

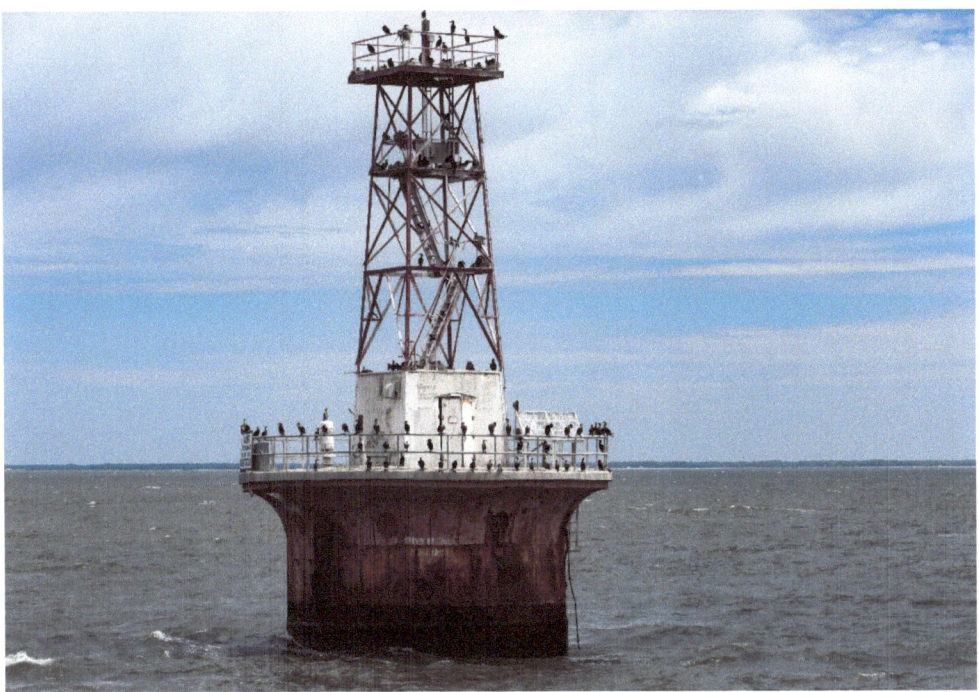

Ship John Shoal

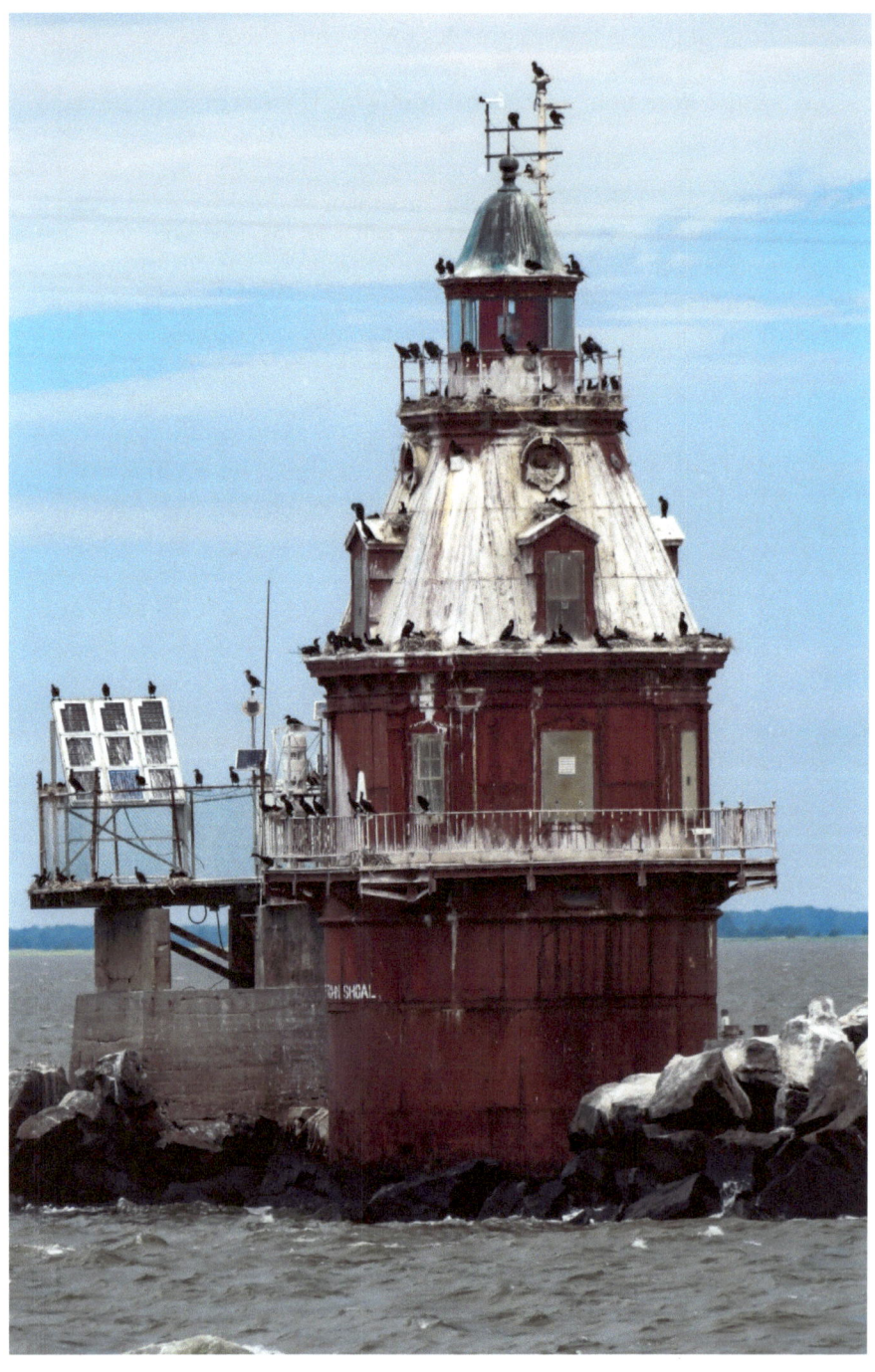

This sparkplug type lighthouse is located very close to the Delaware State line in the middle of Delaware Bay. The shoals are named for the ship *John* that foundered here in 1797 while completing a trip from Hamburg, Germany to Philadelphia, Pennsylvania. Remarkably, no passengers, crew, or cargo was lost and the original figurehead from the ship was salvaged and is now on display at the maritime Museum in Greenwich, New Jersey.

Originally, the lighthouse was to be screw pile design but because screw pile construction was susceptible to damage from ice, a caisson was ultimately chosen since that technology had improved. The first caisson was constructed in 1874; however, construction of the light was incomplete. A temporary light was in service until completion of the permanent structure.

The incomplete construction led to two interesting quirks about this lighthouse. First, the original superstructure designed for the site ended up as the *Southwest Ledge Light* in Connecticut. The second replacement superstructure became an exhibit at the *Centennial Exhibition* held in nearby Philadelphia in 1876. It wasn't until 1887 that the light found its home on the base located at the present site.

The original station featured a fourth-order Fresnel lens and was manned until 1973 when the US Coast Guard automated the light. The current lens is a VRB-25 with a range of 16 nautical miles.

In 2011, Ship John Shoal Light was declared excess and offered to preservation groups for free. When no group came forward, the light was put on the auction block and was sold in 2012 for $60,200.

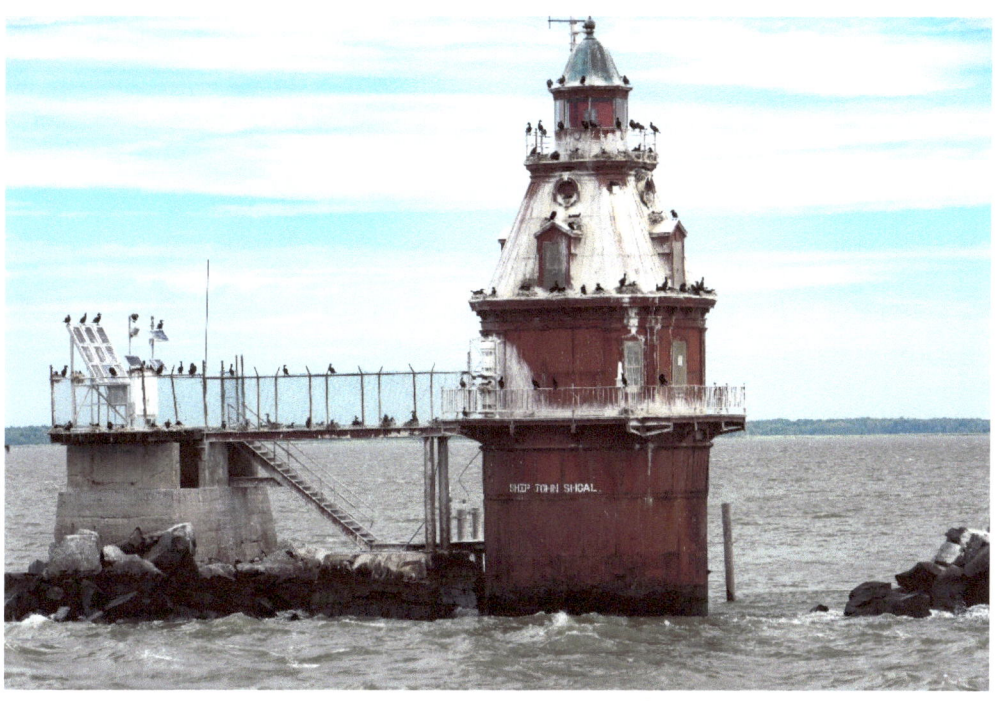

Finn's Point Rear Range

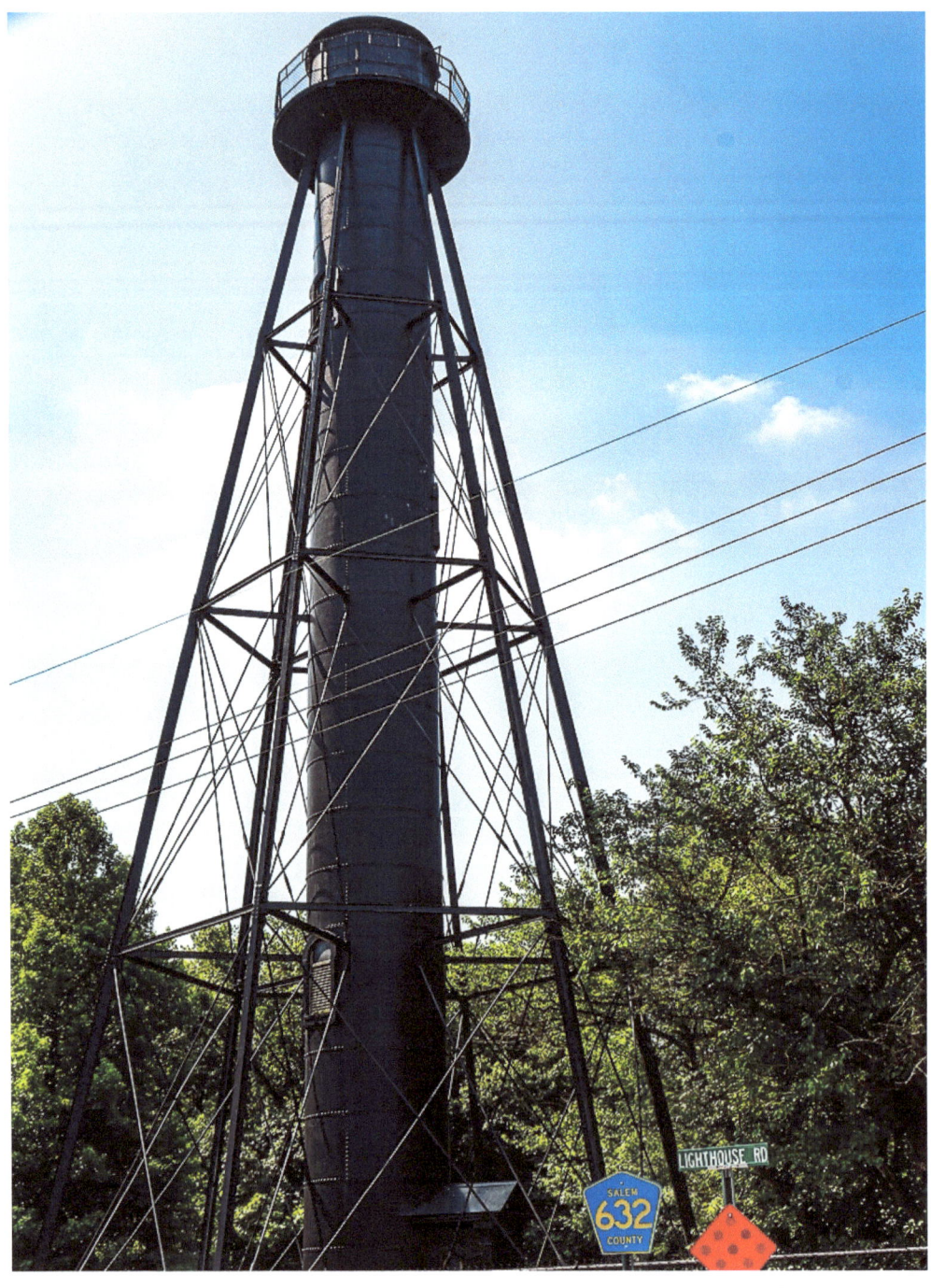

This lighthouse is a cast iron skeleton structure about 1.5 miles inland from riverbank. Finn's Point Rear Range was part of a two lighthouse arrangement that led seafarers into the Delaware River from Delaware Bay. The front range lighthouse is no longer in existence having been torn down in 1939.

The Finn's Point Rear Range was completed in 1877 and shone through 1933; however, complaints from mariners forced the government to relight the lighthouse in 1939. The original lens was a fourth order Fresnel lens. The light is not currently operational.

After work completed in the channel leading to the Delaware River made the light unnecessary, the light was closed in 1952. The grounds were essentially abandoned and much deterioration of both the remaining structures of the front range campus and the rear range suffered. Locals, concerned about the future of the lighthouse, made a successful bid to have the remaining rear range tower added to the National Register of Historic Sites in 1978. Through their efforts, funds to restore the lighthouse bore fruit in 1984 and the tower was reopened to the public. By 2008 the tower was closed to the public as funding lapsed but another campaign saw the tower reopen in 2013 on a limited basis as it now resides within a National Wildlife Refuge.

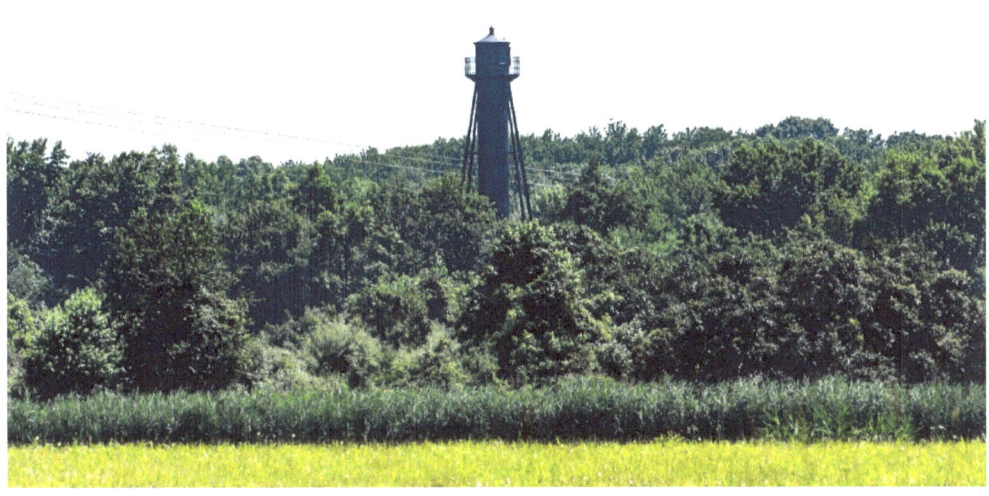

Tinicum Island Rear Range

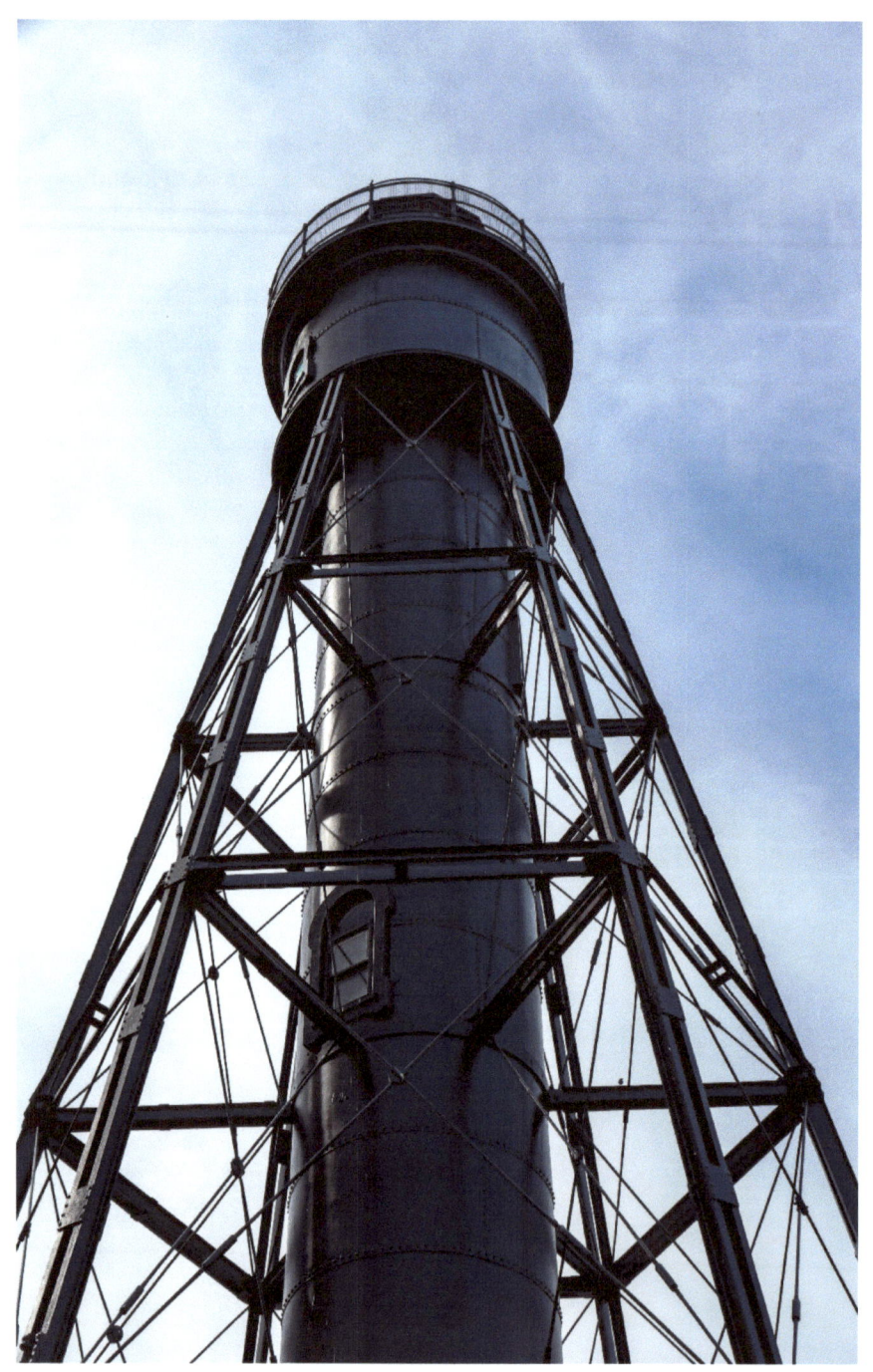

Tinicum Island Rear Range is one of a trio of lights that mark the Delaware River south of Philadelphia, PA. This light worked in conjunction with the Billingsport Front Light and Fort Mifflin Bar Range Light.

First lit in 1880, the light had a range of 8.5 nautical miles. The United States Coast Guard automated the light in 1933. The lighthouse is a skeleton type constructed of steel. The light was originally red, changed to white and then back to fixed red.

The campus originally had the light tower, a dwelling, oil house, barn, and miscellaneous structures but the out buildings were razed in the 1950s as they fell into disrepair.

The tower is 85 feet tall and remains an active aid to navigation.

The site is maintained by the *Tinicum Rear Range Lighthouse Society* and is open to the public on the third Sunday of the month from April to September and the third weekend of October. Climbing to the top offers views of the City of Philadelphia across the Delaware River and its international airport.

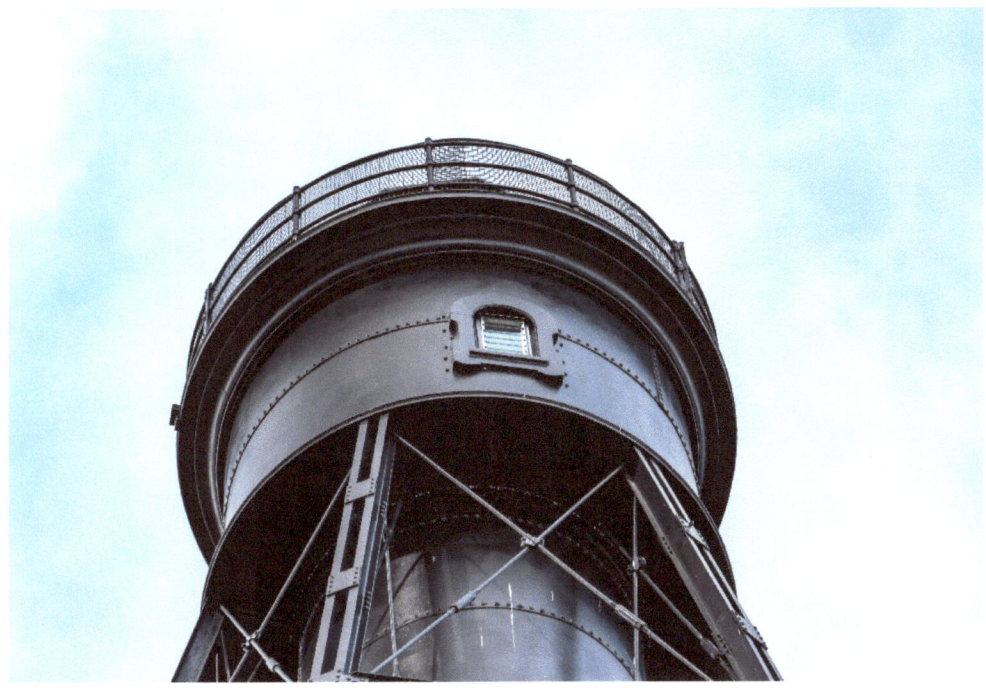

Fresnel Lens

In any discussion about lighthouses you will see references to Fresnel Lenses (pronounced *fray NEL*) but why are the references there?

The Fresnel Lens is an important part of lighthouse evolution that brought the technology to the highest levels. Without getting into the physics of lens design, the Fresnel Lens is a focusing magnifying glass just like the magnifying glasses that you might have played with as a child. Your childhood magnifying glass was a simple convex lens of single piece of glass or plastic. The light accumulates on the glass but the convex design lets the light rays focus into a single point.

In a similar way, light emanating from a single point can be focused into parallel rays through a lens. This is the basic concept of a lighthouse. Light originating in the lighthouse is broadcast outward from a single point.

Using conventional lenses to focus the light into narrow beams that could be seen for many miles at sea required either brighter light sources or larger and heavier lenses to broadcast the light. Achieving both was a challenge in the 19th Century.

Augustin Fresnel, a French physicist, is credited with the idea of reducing the size and weight of a conventional lens by using an assortment of prisms that effectively focused and thus amplified the light into a narrow beam. His invention was first used at the Cordouan lighthouse in France in 1823 and produced a light visible for 20 miles.

Another reference in many books about lighthouses regarding Fresnel lenses is their order. You will see first-order, second-order, etc. Fresnel lenses were installed in various lighthouses with different order lenses.

The order of a lens describes its size and focal length. There are 11 orders from Eight Order to Hyperadial, however, Fresnel himself only originally designed and installed six lens sizes in four orders.

Modern optics uses the same basic technology used by Fresnel including in the lenses used to take the photographs in this book. The lens designers can make lighter and more efficient lenses by incorporating the Fresnel design elements with computer assisted milling and machining.

National Register of Historical Places

The National Park Service manages a database of historic properties throughout the United States. Below are the lighthouses of New Jersey and of those listed on the register the year that they were added and their reference number. The significance of each light may fall into multiple categories such as transportation, architecture, or communications therefore multiple periods may be listed. Please see the National Register of Historic Places for more details.

Lighthouse	Year Added	Number	Period(s) of Significance
Absecon	1971	71000492	1900-1924 1875-1899 1850-1874
Barnegat	1971	71000512	1900-1924 1875-1899 1850-1874 1925-1949
Brandywine Shoals	2007	06000943	1900-1924 1925-1949 1950-1974
Cape May	1973	73001090	1850-1874
Chapel Hill	Not Listed		
Conover Beacon	Not Listed		
East Point	Not Listed		
Elbow of Cross Ledge	Not Listed		
Finn's Point Rear Range	1978	78001792	1875-1899
Great Beds	2008	08000467	1875-1899 1900-1924 1925-1949 1950-1974
Hereford Inlet	1977	77000859	1850-1874
Miah Maull	1991	90002188	1900-1924
Robbins Reef	2006	06000631	1825-1849 1850-1874 1875-1899 1900-1924 1925-1949 1950-1974
Romer Shoal	2007	06001304	1875-1899 1900-1924 1925-1949 1950-1974

Sandy Hook	1966	66000468	1750-1799
Sea Girt	Not Listed		
Ship John Shoal	2006	060000630	1850-1874
			1875-1899
			1900-1924
			1925-1949
			1950-1974
Tinicum Island Rear Range	2005	05001053	1875-1899
			1900-1924
			1925-1949
			1950-1974
Tucker's Island	Not Listed		
Twin Lights	1970	70000389	1875-1899
			1850-1874
			1825-1849

About the Author

Michelangelo DeSantis is a native of Brooklyn, New York but has lived for more than 30 years in Manalapan, New Jersey. He combines his love for history with the twin passions of travel and photography. This is his second book. His first, *The Jersey Shore*, is a photographic essay through all of the towns along the New Jersey shore.

His photographic work has been shown at the Monmouth County Library and he has won multiple awards for photos in various on-line communities. Michelangelo is a contributor to Shutterstock, Adobe Stock, and Wildlife Reference Photos for Artists.

His next project is a collaborative effort with his wife, Denise. The subject of the work is *The Missions of California*.

www.ingramcontent.com/pod-product-compliance
Lightning Source LLC
Chambersburg PA
CBHW051222220526
45473CB00003B/1139